# HAGADDAH
## FOR
# PASSOVER

# T'FILAH L'ANI

**With meditations from
The Ari Z"l, HaRashash, HaRamchal,
Ha'Ba'al Shem Tov, and HaRich**

by
# Kabbalist Rav Berg Shlita
**Director of
Yeshivat Kol Yehudah**

**Edited
by his son**
# Rabbi Yehudah Berg Shlita

Published by
The Kabbalah Centre International Inc.


155 E. 48th St., New York, NY 10017
1062 S. Robertson Blvd., Los Angeles, CA 90035

Director Rav Berg

First printing 2000
Second printing 2004

Printed in USA

ISBN: 1-57189-029-7

WINE
BINAH
LOVES
⊕ ⊖

MATZAH
CHOCHMAH
FETUS
⊕ ⊖

—GADLUT
BET—
↑ 15 steps

May the letters on this paper find the unity of

the Last Supper and the Passover celebration,

bringing us together with the common goal of

eliminating chaos, by slaughtering our egos.

—Inspired by Abe Altman

### FIELD OF DREAMS

Imagine gathering eighteen people onto a baseball diamond. Each one of them is blessed with enormous skill and talent, on the level of Babe Ruth, Sandy Koufax and Mark MacGuire.

Suppose they were given the equipment to play the game. Except one thing is missing – the rules. None of them have a clue as to what baseball is, or how to play. Imagine what would happen if they were not allowed to leave the field until they completed one game? The result would be utter chaos - fighting, screaming, frustration, quitting. On the other hand, once given the rules, these 18 people would evolve into magnificent ball players.

There is a game a lot older than the game of baseball. It is called life. And the rules to this most challenging game were recorded in an ancient manuscript some 2000 years ago. The rulebook is called the Zohar, the definitive body of knowledge on Kabbalah.

There are two golden rules to this game of life according to the Zohar. Before we reveal them, let us first learn how and why this game came into existence.

### LIFE, ACCORDING TO KABBALAH

Before the origin of our physical universe, there was an infinite expanse of energy. This energy reached as far as forever. The nature of this energy force was sharing. Its essence was infinite fulfillment.

This boundless force of energy is oftentimes called God. The enlightened Kabbalists preferred to call this energy force, the Light. Two reasons:

1. As the light of a bulb instantly expands and fills a darkened room, this Light expands and fills all infinity.
2. As white sunlight contains all the colors of the spectrum, the Light contains every type of fulfillment one could possibly desire.

### THE CREATION OF THE VESSEL

To express its nature of sharing, the Light created a receiver, a vessel, in order to impart all of Its fulfillment. This Vessel's sole nature was an infinite *desire to receive*. In other words, for every type of pleasure issued forth by the Light, there was a corresponding *desire to receive* inside the Vessel.

This realm of Light and Vessel is called the Endless World.

The Vessel is also known by a code name. Chances are, you've already heard of it -- the code name for the Vessel is *Adam*. All the souls of humanity throughout time were a part of the original Vessel/Adam. We were one soul in the same way that the seven colors of the rainbow are unified within a beam of white sunlight.

### GOD'S DNA

When the Light created the Vessel, the Vessel inherited the attributes of its Creator, one of which was sharing. In the Endless World, the Vessel had no one to share with consequently, the Vessel could not express its "inherited" God-like feature.

This inability prevented the Vessel from experiencing total fulfillment, which created somewhat of a problem because experiencing total fulfillment was the reason why the Vessel was created in the first place.

That's when something rather remarkable happened: The Vessel *stopped* receiving the Light for the opportunity and chance to express its own sharing nature.

This act of refusing the Light triggered the Big Bang origins of our universe. Like a loving parent who stands back to allow their child to fall so that the child will ultimately learn to walk on his own, the Light withdrew Its radiance and created a vacated space the instant that the Vessel said "Thanks, but no thanks. I'd like to generate a little Light on my own."

In the same way that a loving father steps aside to allow his son the freedom to learn the family business so eventually the young man can take it over with a sense of accomplishment, the Light gave the Vessel the space [literally speaking] to learn how to evolve its inherent Godly-nature of sharing.

In a process, whose description lies beyond the scope of this Hagaddah, the one infinite Vessel then shattered into endless pieces of all sizes and grades. All the matter in our universe -- from atoms to zebras, from microbes to musicians -- is a piece of the original Vessel. Each represents a different level of a *desire to receive.*

The only difference between a pebble and a person is the degree of their *desire to receive* Light. That is what a Vessel does. It receives Light. The more Light it receives, the more complex the entity. The more complex the entity, the higher the consciousness. A human being is more complex than an ant. A cow possesses a higher state of consciousness than a rock.

## THE MEANING OF LIFE

You, along with everyone else on this planet, are part of the Vessel. And we came here to learn how to become God, to unleash our Godly nature embedded in the DNA of our soul. We can achieve that transformation through our interactions with each other in the game of life.

Our purpose in this world, [though 99.9% of the world doesn't know it] is to transform our reactive nature of receiving selfishly for reasons that serve our own ego and self-interest, into the proactive nature of receiving for the sake of sharing with others. And though it may sound like a simple and noble enough task, it is one that requires near super-human will power and self-restraint.

Now why is that? Why is it so much easier to react in anger than to turn the other cheek and be proactive? Why is greed more fun than generosity?

## THE FORCE OF RESISTENCE

To strengthen muscle tissue when exercising, there must be resistance. Likewise, strengthening our "sharing muscle" also requires a force of resistance. To help us evolve and strengthen our undeveloped God-like muscle, the Light created a force of resistance to challenge us every step of the way.

This opposing force of resistance is known by the code word *Satan*, otherwise known as the Evil Inclination. However you choose to call it, the force called Satan was first revealed in the writings of the ancient Kabbalists some 2000 years ago. Satan is not the character who wears a red suit, wields pitchfork and sports two shiny horns. His is an intelligent force of resistance that resides in our rational conscious mind and whispers, "Do it" even though we know we shouldn't. He murmurs "Don't" every time we know we should.

The name of this force eventually spread to the other religions of the world. In the process, confusion set in concerning the true nature of this force leading to superstition, myth and folklore. The result -- we forgot who the real opponent was in this game called Life.

The Satan is best identified as our instinctive, reactive, egocentric nature. The purpose of our opponent is to stimulate reactions within us. All those negative impulses you thought were yours, well, they weren't. Your competitiveness, envy, fear, insecurity, they are all different expressions of Satan, like various sized weights on a barbell for you to resist as you train for this game of life. Each time we resist our urge to react, we strengthen our

God-muscle. We play the game better. Conversely, each time we succumb to our desire to react, we weaken ourselves and strengthen this negative force called Satan. The game becomes more difficult.

### THE POWER OF DARKNESS

A question we might ask is this: why did the Vessel have to shatter and descend into this physical universe to change its nature? Why could the Vessel not learn to share while living in the blazing radiance of the Endless World? Two reason: one, the vessel had no one to share with so it split up into various pieces so that it could learn to share with itself. But it doesn't know that. Wearing the masquerade costume called *ego*, we don't recognize ourselves in others. This way, sharing and changing ourselves becomes a difficult, and therefore, worthy task.

Second, just as a lit candle has no real worth or value on a sunlit day, the Vessel could not express sharing in a realm already radiating infinite beneficence. So the Light set up a series of curtains -- ten to be exact -- to gradually dim the intensity of Its luminescence. These ten curtains are called the *Ten Sfirot*. With the glimmer of Light reduced to the minimum level of illumination, the Vessel has an arena where it can learn to master the God-like art of sharing.

The only remnant of Light remaining in this darkened universe is a "pilot light" that sustains our existence. This "pilot light" is the life force of a human being and the force that gives birth to stars, sustains suns and sets galaxies in motion.

### THE RULES

The two golden rules in this game are as follows:

1. We remove chaos and achieve lasting fulfillment each time we transform our reactive desires into a proactive desire to share with others. We achieve temporary gratification coupled with eventual long-term chaos whenever we react.

2. Love thy neighbor as thyself or at least treat your friends and enemies with human dignity.

### THE WEAPONS OF SATAN

To make the game more challenging, Satan was given a few extra weapons. One of those weapons is called *time*. Satan uses *time* to separate cause and effect. In other words, if we react and behave negatively, Satan uses *time* to delay the inevitable consequences. This *time delay* confuses us. We start thinking that we are actually getting away with our wrongful actions.

Likewise, when we stop our reactions and become proactive sharing people, the fulfillment owing to us is also deferred by time. We start believing that good behavior goes unrewarded.

To compound the confusion, the next time we react negatively, Satan manipulates time once more and rewards us with the fulfillment that we earned from a prior positive deed. We begin to associate reactive behavior with pleasure. It appears as though selfish behavior generates fulfillment while good behavior produces chaos.

Satan can delay the consequences of our actions for months, years, decades or even lifetimes. The result? Life appears to be one random, chaotic mess!

A brilliant and potent strategy, indeed.

## THE PURPOSE OF PESACH

Immediately upon our arrival in this physical world, the Satan quickly gained the upper hand in the game of life. In other words, he helped us become a species totally governed by ego and reactive instincts.

It was this reactive behavior, induced by the Satan, that became the source and wellspring of all the chaos that strikes our world. Chaos refers to both global and personal turmoil. From poverty, disease and earthquakes, to personal stress, fear, and lousy relationships, Satan was and is the unseen and unknown cause behind it all.

Satan has one secret that he doesn't want us to know about: He has absolutely no power or Light of his own. He appropriates all his Light from our reactive behavior.

The truth is, humanity didn't stand a chance in the early rounds of the game.

It was equivalent to sending an amateur lightweight boxer into the ring with a world champion heavyweight.

Humanity was on the ropes. Ego, greed, self-indulgence, envy and hatred preoccupied the minds of men. Satan toyed with a person for 50 years, building up his ego, rewarding him with illusions. All this stimulated reactive behavior, the life force of Satan.

Like any good predator, he fattened up his prey, giving them wealth, pride, the illusion of control, and when they least expected, he pulled the rug out. That technique produced the greatest negative reactions of all in a person. Those reactions gave Satan the strength he needed for the final deathblow.

During the time of Egypt, the game reached a critical point. Satan was in complete control. He had a stranglehold on us and there was no way for us to win. This is the spiritual significance and code concealed inside the story of the Israelites slavery in Egypt.

Egypt is a code word for our ego and reactive behavior. Slavery refers to Satan's complete domination over humanity. We were going down for the count. And that's when something remarkable happened. The Light intervened on our behalf. This is the power of Passover.

Suddenly, 10 massive jolts of spiritual energy [signified by the code term "10 Plagues"] were thrust into our world. The shockwave sent Satan reeling. His grip of death was broken. Suddenly, we found ourselves on equal footing with our opponent. The moment his stranglehold was broken, chaos vanquished. This is signified by the Israelites exodus from Egypt and the state of immortality that was achieved on Mount Sinai.

The Kabbalists teach us that this was not the end of Satan. It was merely a chance for us to regain our footing and level the playing field. If we reacted again, Satan could continue to drain us of our Light.

## THE SEDER

All these historic spiritual actions of Passover served a purpose designed to benefit our life today. They created a reservoir and bank of spiritual energy that future generations could tap for their own battles with Satan. Therein lies the purpose of the seder.

The seder plate is a microcosm of our life and the physical and spiritual world.

We are the plate and the items on it correlate to the 10 Sfirot and the 10 blasts of energy that struck our world back in Egypt. Each component on the seder plate is a specific tool and instrument that allow us to manipulate these 10 spiritual forces.

In our own personal life, all year long, the Satan literally has us in a death grip. He controls our every thought, desire and impulse, making it virtually impossible for us to transform our nature. He is so powerful, he can even instill doubts within us concerning the reality of his existence or the truth of all these Kabbalistic explanations.

Our actions on Passover generate enough raw naked energy to pummel Satan with massive amounts of spiritual current. We break his stranglehold and start the rest of the year off on equal footing. With Satan shocked and dazed, we have effectively removed any and all chaos from our life since it is Satan who is the source of all turmoil.

His only chance for a comeback is renewed strength. That can only happen if we give it to him through our reactive insensitive behavior.

Remember that Satan has absolutely no power of his own. He embezzles all his Light from our reactive behavior. Satan has to feed and nourish just as we do. He is the one entity in this world with which we should not share.

Tonight, we break the grip of death, end chaos and even the score.

Tomorrow, it's up to us carry through with our work by maintaining a spiritual consciousness.

## THE SEDER PLATE

The items that appear on the Seder Plate, when charged with the energy of Pesach become highly sophisticated instruments that connect us to various levels of the *Ten Sfirot* - the Kabbalistic Tree of Life, see appendix.

## CHOCHMA, BINAH AND DA'AT

The three Matzot link us to the three upper *Sfirot*: *Chochmah*, *Binah* and *Da'at*[1]. These Upper Three are the source of all the fulfillment and goodness that appears in our life.

Moshe was the only human being ever to attain the level of *Da'at*. The Kabbalists say that he was half man and half angel. It might be assumed that he achieved the status of the greatest prophet that ever lived as a result of his angel nature. However, the Kabbalists teach us that the true greatness of Moshe was the part of him that was half man. As a man, Moshe cared for every single human being. He was willing to give of himself and help anyone, on an individual basis. Although he was the leader of an entire nation, he had the heart, soul and mind set to consider and care for the needs of every person.

No matter how spiritually elevated we become in life, we can never be too high to reach out to people - regardless what level we think they are on. In fact, when a person reaches a high level of spirituality, care and consideration for everyone and anyone is automatic. It is that concern that elevates a person in the first place. We can use this as measure of our own spiritual level. If we think that we are above or more important than any other person, then we have not achieved an elevated state of spirituality.

## CHESED

Our first connection to the Seder Plate involves the shank bone or a piece of burnt meat. This signifies the sacrifice that was brought to the Temple during Pesach and corresponds to the *Sfirah* of *Chesed*. The level of *Chesed* represents and is contained in water and in actions of sharing, giving, and mercy. What is the relationship to the slaughtering of an animal?

According to the Kabbalists, in order to really share, we need to sacrifice and relinquish our own negative characteristics. Because we can only share what we have, by ridding ourselves of our negative qualities we can share all our positive energy with others.

## GVURAH

The egg, unfortunately signifies the Israel nation (The longer we boil an egg the harder it becomes.) It also represents the level of energy known as *Gvurah*. *Gvurah* can break this pattern. All of us cling to our own opinions and ideas. The more people oppose us the harder we become and the more entrenched we are in our own ideas. We usually sacrifice the good of a situation if it serves to validate and strengthen our own position. Our nature is to expend as much energy as possible in order to prove our point - to be right at all costs. By making this connection we can master the valuable art of conceding. We gain the discipline to listen and learn from our adversaries in life. We get the strength and the wisdom to let go of our own ideas and accept opposing views that might actually serve the common good. This connection softens our resolve in situations where our stubborn inclination actually hurts us and the people in our life.

---

1. *Da'at* is a unique *Sfirah*, and is not considered to be part of the *Ten Sfirot*. The purpose of *Da'at* is to collect the raw naked energy from the *Upper Three* - *Keter*, *Chochmah* and *Binah* and combine them into one force that is transferred into the lower seven *Sfirot*. *Da'at* functions more like a way-station than an actual *Sfirah*.

## TIFERET

The *Sfirah* of *Tiferet* is central column - the balance between right and left. *Maror* -raw horseradish (extra strength) is our connection to this energy of balance. On the surface, *Maror* seems to be a harsh tool because of its pungent flavor and sensation of death. However, if we truly want to achieve something of spiritual importance in this world, we must endure a process[2] that involves challenge and discomfort. For some of us, this process is short lived, for others, it takes a lifetime. All the pain, suffering and torment that we endure in life, in whatever measure, is part of that process. We can, however, shorten or lengthen this process by our actions. If we bring more spiritual balance into our lives we automatically shorten the process. If we are unbalanced, tilted towards reactive behavior, we extend the process. When we eat from the bitter herb *Maror*, we experience a taste of death in a proactive way and shorten our own *Tikkun process*, thereby removing chaos from our life.

There is another lesson for us: many times, when we are jealous of others, we look only at the final result of what a person possesses. But do we really stop and consider the process they had to undergo in order to achieve their results? If we could observe the entire picture, we would learn to appreciate everything in our own life.

## NETZACH

The connection to the *Sfirah* of *Netzach* is represented by a unique blend of fruits and spices called *Charoset*. This jam-like substance was formulated by 16th century, Kabbalist Rabbi Isaac Luria. Embedded in the name *Charoset*, we find the name Ruth (וֹס(ארות), a maternal ancestor of King David. One of Ruth's ancestors was Moav, a man born out of an incestuous relationship between a father and daughter. Because of her ancestry, Ruth could have easily chosen a path where she had no chance to bring any spiritual Light into the world, but instead she made choices which lead her to give birth to King David who is the seed of the *Mashiach*. What is the Torah trying to teach us with this story? No matter how sordid or shameful our past maybe, we can still rise to great spiritual heights the moment we make the decision and commitment to do so. When we eat from the *Charoset* we are imbued with the strength to make that commitment.

## HOD

The *Karpas* [celery or parsley] connects us to the realm of *Hod*.
We can rearrange the letters of the word *Karpas* as follows: ס פּרך

The phrase *Samech Perakh* refers to the hard work of the 600,000 people in Egypt. The concept of hard work during captivity, is a metaphor for judgment. We dip the *Karpas* into salt water to sweeten any and all judgments coming our way in the following year. According to Kabbalah, salt is a positive force, water embodies the aspect of mercy and blood contains the force of judgment. Here is how it all ties together: The hemoglobin in our blood is a salt-like saline solution. The spiritual force behind the salt and the water

---

2. This is known in Kabbalistic terms as the *Tikkun Process* and refers to the specific corrections each of us has to make in our lifetime. These spiritual corrections are based upon negative deeds committed in this life and past lives. Any hardship we encounter, any pain or difficulty we endure is part of our *Tikkun Process*. It gives us the opportunity to correct reactive deeds of the past, by not reacting in the present. If we do react, we will encounter the same hardship over and over again until we finally fix the problem. Here is the challenge: the Satan will employ all his powers to stimulate reactions in us during our *Tikkun process*. Satan has an almost unbreakable stranglehold on us, which he uses to ignite emotional and physical reactions. Pesach loosens this death grip so that we can arouse inner strength to stop our reactions.

connects to the hemoglobin in our blood. The moment we eat the *Karpas* we sweeten any judgments that might be hanging over us[3].

## YESOD

The connection to *Yesod* is called *Chazeret* and is represented on the Seder Plate by Romaine lettuce. *Yesod* is a reservoir that collects all the energy from all the *Sfirot* above it. Kabbalah explains that the biblical character, Yosef the Righteous, represents the *Sfira* of *Yesod*. While he was alive, Yosef accumulated all the wealth of the world in Egypt and dispersed it throughout the land. Yosef accomplishes this in the spiritual realm as well through *Yesod*. We utilize this same power to accumulate all of our negative traits and all the chaos that appears in our life and combine it into one single target. Now we can wipe out and remove all the chaos of life with one single shot from Pesach.

## MALCHUT

The physical plate is our connection to *Malchut*, which corresponds to our material existence. The plate itself has no spiritual value. The spiritual commodities residing on it determine the plate's value. Likewise, we have no spiritual sustenance of our own in this physical world. We derive all our spiritual energy from the *Sfirot* that we connect to via the items on our Seder Plate[4].

---

3. Judgments are not necessarily a bad thing. Judgments can also have a positive effect as it helps direct us towards a more spiritual way of life [provided we learn from our hardships and recognize the cause and effect principle at work in the universe]. For example, a loving parent reprimanding their child for misbehavior is productive, sweetened judgment. Conversely, any kind of personal tragedy is judgment that is harsh, lacking any form of sweetening. Our connection to the *Charoset* sweetens all the judgments that are due us as a result of past negative deeds.

4. The Seder Plate is a microcosm of our life and the physical and spiritual world. We are the plate and the items on it correlate to the *10 Sfirot* in the upper worlds. Each component on the Seder plate is a specific tool and instrument that allow us to manipulate the spiritual forces that govern the cosmos. By controlling the *10 Sfirot*, we are seizing control of the power station for the entire universe. As we learned earlier, throughout our year, Satan literally has us in a death grip. He controls our every thought, desire and impulse, making it virtually impossible for us to transform our nature. He is so powerful, he can even instill us with doubts about his existence or the truth of this explanation. By taking control over the power station we can crank up the output and flow of energy. This generates raw naked energy, enough power to shock Satan with massive amounts of spiritual current. The jolt sends him reeling. His stranglehold is broken and we start the rest of the year off on equal footing. Here is the additional payoff: with Satan stunned, we have effectively removed any and all chaos from our life since it is Satan who is the source of all negativity and turmoil. His only chance for a comeback and renewed strength is if we empower him with our negative reactions. Kabbalah teaches us that Satan has absolutely no power or Light of his own. He appropriates all his Light from our reactive behavior. Satan has to feed and nourish just as we do. He is the one entity in this world with whom we should not share.

# סֵדֶר הַקְּעָרָה לְדֵעַת רַבִּינוּ הָאֲרִיזַ"ל:

*The proper arrangement of the Seder plate, according to the Ari, is shown below.*

## וֹזכמה בּינה דֵעַת

*Chochmah Binah Da'at*

# שָׁלוֹש מַצוֹת

*Three Matzas*

| גְבוּרָה | | וֹזסד |
|---|---|---|
| *Gvurah* | | *Chesed* |
| בֵּיצָה | | זֵרוֹע |
| *An Egg* | | *A Scorched Chicken Throat* |

### תִּפְאֶרֶת

*Tiferet*

### מָרוֹר

*Bitter Herbs (Horseradish)*

| הוֹד | | נֵצַח |
|---|---|---|
| *Hod* | | *Netzach* |
| כרפּס | | וֹזרוֹסת |
| *Celery/Parsley* | | *Fruit Blend* |

### יְסוֹד

*Yesod*

### וֹזֶרֶת

*Lettuce*

### מַלְכוּת

*Malchut*

### וְהַקְּעָרָה

*The Seder Plate Itself*

קַדֵּשׁ. וּרְחַץ. כַּרְפַּס. יַחַץ. מַגִּיד. רָחְצָה. מוֹצִיא. מַצָּה. מָרוֹר. כּוֹרֵךְ.
שֻׁלְחָן עוֹרֵךְ. צָפוּן. בָּרֵךְ. הַלֵּל ללה. נִרְצָה.

*No silliness here
Maintain your
Consciousness*

*silly - Rationalize
why it's ok
even when we
know otherwise*

*Lean to
left*

*gadlut Bet
transforms
our negative
Loves*

## STAGE ONE: THE KADESH
### THE FIRST CUP OF WINE: ATZILUT

# קַדֵּשׁ

There are four cups of wine poured during the Seder. These signify and connect us to the four-letter name of God – the Tetragrammaton[5] – and four Upper Worlds in our spiritual atmosphere. The names of these worlds are Atzilut, Briyah, Yetzirah, and Asiyah.

### L'SHEM YICHUD

L'Shem Yichud attempts to unify our thoughts and our actions. Many times we have a thought to do the right thing, but when it comes time, our actions are the complete opposite of our original thought and intention. Dieting and exercising are prime examples.

This connection unifies our thoughts and actions, and for that important reason, it precedes the prayers.

Throughout the process we will, we hope, make a conscious effort to improve ourselves spiritually. L'shem Yichud will help keep us true to our positive thoughts and intentions, especially the day after the Seder.

לְשֵׁם יִחוּד קוּדְשָׁא בְּרִיךְ הוּא וּשְׁכִינְתֵּיהּ בִּדְחִילוּ וּרְחִימוּ

וּרְחִימוּ וּדְחִילוּ לְיַחֲדָא שֵׁם יוּד קֵי בְּוָאו קֵי בְּיִחוּדָא

שְׁלִים יהוה בְּשֵׁם כָּל יلּ יִשְׂרָאֵל, הִנְנִי מוּכָן וּמְזוּמָּן לְקַיֵּם

מִצְוַת קִידוּשׁ וּמִצְוַת כּוֹס מוء רִאשׁוֹן שֶׁל אַרְבַּע כּוֹסוֹת,

וִיהִי נֹעַם אֲדֹנָי אֱלֹהֵינוּ ילה עָלֵינוּ וּמַעֲשֵׂה יָדֵינוּ כּוֹנְנָה

עָלֵינוּ וּמַעֲשֵׂה יָדֵינוּ כּוֹנְנֵהוּ:

*For the sake of unifying The Holy One, blessed be It, and Its Shechinah, with fear and mercy, and with mercy and fear, to unify the name of Yud Key with Vav Key completely, in the name of all Israel, I am ready and willing to apply the connection of Kiddush and the connection of First Cup out of Four Cups, and may the pleasantness of Hashem, our God, be upon us and establish the action of our hands upon us and establish the action of our hands.*

### Kiddush

*The time of our redemption is now.* What does this verse really mean to us today? Are we merely celebrating an event that occurred more than three millennia ago? In reality, we

---

5. The Tetragrammaton is a powerful combination of Hebrew letters that literally transmits the spiritual forces of the Upper World into our physical existence. The four letters of the Tetragrammaton are יהוה.

are connecting to the energy that brought forth the event of Passover at this precise moment. From a spiritual perspective, the events are happening as we read these words.

Both Moshe and Einstein understood that time is an illusion. Past, present, and future are really connected as one unified whole on a deeper level of reality.[6]

The Kiddush connects us to the idea that there is no time or space. The word *Kiddush* means "holy," which is a code word for the spiritual realm of *Ein Soff,* which means "nothingness." All miracles, freedom, and fulfillment originate from this realm. "Holy" also refers to the word *whole.*

We connect ourselves to the word *holy,* to the world of nothingness and to the word *whole* because *Ein Soff* is a unified realm of complete wholeness. There is no fragmentation, no time, and no separation. Fragmentation creates separation between yesterday and today. Our physical world contains diversity and fragmentation, which is why there is chaos and a second law of thermodynamics that states that all things become increasingly more disordered as time passes.

In the spiritual realm of nothingness, there is only wholeness and unity. There are no such concepts as space or time, leaving no room or no moments for any chaos to set in.

With that understanding, we can now make the leap into the realm of nothingness, transcend time and space, and tap the same power of miracles, freedom, and redemption that occurred more than 3,300 years ago.

---

On Shabbat we start here:

בלחש: וַיְהִי עֶרֶב וַיְהִי בוֹקֶר יוֹם נגד, ן הַשִּׁשִּׁי.

וַיְכֻלּוּ ע״ב שמות הַשָּׁמַיִם י״פ טל וְהָאָרֶץ וְכָל צְבָאָם:

וַיְכַל אֱלֹהִים ילה בַּיּוֹם נגד, ן הַשְּׁבִיעִי מְלַאכְתּוֹ אֲשֶׁר

עָשָׂה וַיִּשְׁבֹּת בַּיּוֹם נגד, ן הַשְּׁבִיעִי מִכָּל מְלַאכְתּוֹ אֲשֶׁר

עָשָׂה: וַיְבָרֶךְ עסמ״ב אֱלֹהִים ילה אֶת יוֹם נגד, ן הַשְּׁבִיעִי

וַיְקַדֵּשׁ אֹתוֹ

(Whispering) *Then there was evening and then there was morning. The sixth day. The heaven and the earth and all their troops were complete. On the seventh day, God finished The work He did, and on the seventh day, He ceased from all work which He did. And God blessed the seventh day and sanctified it,*

---

6.  Time is like a revolving wheel. The same spoke of freedom that occurred 3,000 years ago in Egypt is coming around again tonight. Events do not pass by us like a one-way freight train. We move through the wheel of time, revisiting the same moments each year. The only things that change are the "set decorations" to give us the illusion of a new year and a new life.

כִּי בוֹ שָׁבַת מִכָּל מְלַאכְתּוֹ

אֲשֶׁר בָּרָא קנ"א בּ"ן אֱלֹהִים ילה לַעֲשׂוֹת:

*because in that day He ceased from all Its work, which God created to act.*

On any other day we start here:

סַבְרִי מָרָנָן:

בָּרוּךְ אַתָּה יְהֹוָהאדני־אהדונהי אֱלֹהֵינוּ ילה מֶלֶךְ הָעוֹלָם
בּוֹרֵא פְּרִי הַגָּפֶן:

*With your permission, my masters: Blessed are You, Hashem, our God, King of the universe, Who creates the fruit of the vine.*

בָּרוּךְ אַתָּה יְהֹוָהאדני־אהדונהי אֱלֹהֵינוּ ילה מֶלֶךְ הָעוֹלָם אֲשֶׁר בָּחַר
בָּנוּ מִכָּל עָם וְרוֹמְמָנוּ מִכָּל לָשׁוֹן וְקִדְּשָׁנוּ בְּמִצְוֹתָיו. וַתִּתֶּן־לָנוּ ב"פ
כתת לָנוּ מום יְהֹוָהאדני־אהדונהי אֱלֹהֵינוּ ילה בְּאַהֲבָה אוזר (בשבת: שַׁבָּתוֹת
לִמְנוּחָה וּ) מוֹעֲדִים לְשִׂמְחָה. חַגִּים וּזְמַנִּים לְשָׂשׂוֹן. אֶת יוֹם נגד, ה
(בשבת: הַשַּׁבָּת הַזֶּה והו. וְאֶת יוֹם נגד, ח) וְחַג הַמַּצּוֹת הַזֶּה והו. וְאֶת יוֹם נגד,
ח טוֹב והו מִקְרָא קֹדֶשׁ הַזֶּה והו. זְמַן חֵרוּתֵנוּ. בְּאַהֲבָה אוזר
מִקְרָא קֹדֶשׁ. זֵכֶר לִיצִיאַת מִצְרָיִם מצר: כִּי בָנוּ בָחַרְתָּ
וְאוֹתָנוּ קִדַּשְׁתָּ מִכָּל הָעַמִּים. (בשבת: וְשַׁבָּתוֹת וּ) מוֹעֲדֵי קָדְשֶׁךָ
(בשבת: בְּאַהֲבָה אוזר וּבְרָצוֹן מהש) בְּשִׂמְחָה וּבְשָׂשׂוֹן הִנְחַלְתָּנוּ.

*Blessed are You, Hashem, our God, King of the universe, Who has chosen us from all nations, exalted us above all tongues, and sanctified us with its communications. And You, Hashem, our God, have lovingly given us: (on Saturday we add: Sabbaths for rest) appointed times for gladness, feasts and times for joy, (on Saturday we add: this Shabbat and) this Feast of Matzot, the time of our freedom, with love, holy reading, in memorial of the Exodus from Egypt. For You have chosen and sanctified us above all peoples, (on Saturday we add: and Sabbaths and) Your holy festivals (on Saturday we add: in love and favor) in gladness and joy have You granted us.*

בָּרוּךְ אַתָּה יְהֹוָֽה(אהדי:אהדונהי) מְקַדֵּשׁ (בשבת: הַשַּׁבָּת וְ) יִשְׂרָאֵל וְהַזְּמַנִּים:

*Blessed are You, Hashem, who sanctifies (on Saturday we add: the Sabbath and) Israel and the festive times.*

בָּרוּךְ אַתָּה יְהֹוָֽה(אהדי:אהדונהי) אֱלֹהֵֽינוּ (ילה) מֶֽלֶךְ הָעוֹלָם שֶׁהֶחֱיָֽנוּ וְקִיְּמָֽנוּ וְהִגִּיעָֽנוּ לַזְּמַן הַזֶּה (והו):

*Blessed are You, Hashem, our God, King of the universe Who has kept us alive, sustained us, and brought us to this moment.*

We drink while leaning to the left.

---

### HAVDALLAH

When Passover falls on the Shabbat, we do Havdallah. Many times the people we think are our friends are actually our enemies, while the people we think are our enemies are actually our friends. If we share personal and intimate information about ourselves with our so-called friends, should they ever become our enemies, they will be the most dangerous kind of enemies. Therefore, knowing how to differentiate between good and evil is vital if we are to achieve a sense of peace and serenity in our lives. We are now gaining deeper understanding, insight, and greater awareness about what is good and bad for our personal life.

בָּרוּךְ אַתָּה יְהֹוָֽה(אהדי:אהדונהי) אֱלֹהֵֽינוּ (ילה) מֶֽלֶךְ הָעוֹלָם בּוֹרֵא מְאוֹרֵי הָאֵשׁ (סאה):

*Blessed are You, Hashem, our God, King of the universe, Who creates the illumination of the fire.*

בָּרוּךְ אַתָּה יְהֹוָֽה(אהדי:אהדונהי) אֱלֹהֵֽינוּ (ילה) מֶֽלֶךְ הָעוֹלָם הַמַּבְדִּיל בֵּין קֹֽדֶשׁ לְחוֹל וּבֵין אוֹר (הו) לְחֹשֶׁךְ (וּשׁר), וּבֵין יִשְׂרָאֵל לָעַמִּים, וּבֵין יוֹם (נגד, זן) הַשְּׁבִיעִי לְשֵֽׁשֶׁת יְמֵי הַמַּעֲשֶׂה. בֵּין קְדֻשַּׁת שַׁבָּת לִקְדֻשַּׁת יוֹם (נגד, זן) טוֹב (והו) הִבְדַּֽלְתָּ.

*Blessed are You, Hashem, our God, King of the universe, Who differentiates between sacred and secular, between light and darkness, between Israel and the nations, and between the seventh day and the six days of action. Between the Holy Shabbat and the Holiday You differentiated.*

וְאֶת יוֹם נּה, הַ הַשְּׁבִיעִי מִשֵּׁשֶׁת יְמֵי הַמַּעֲשֶׂה הִקְדַּשְׁתָּ.
וְהִבְדַּלְתָּ וְהִקְדַּשְׁתָּ אֶת עַמְּךָ יִשְׂרָאֵל בִּקְדֻשָּׁתֶךָ:
בָּרוּךְ אַתָּה יְהֹוָאדְהֹוָ אַהִילֹ הַמַּבְדִּיל בֵּין קֹדֶשׁ לְקֹדֶשׁ:

*And between the Seventh day from the six days of action You had sanctified. And distinguished and had sanctified Your Nation, Israel, with Your sanctity. Blessed are You, Hashem, differentiating between the holiness of the Shabbat and the holiness of a festival.*

### STAGE TWO: URCHATZ
### Washing of the Hands

We wash our hands without a blessing.

The Hebrew word *Urchatz* has the same letters as does the Hebrew word *Rotzeach* רוֹצֵחַ, which means "murderer." We want to murder and destroy the negative forces that create havoc in our lives. We can annihilate all the negativity from ourselves and from various things that directly affect us in our environment by pouring water over our hands.

Hands represent judgment and negativity because they carry out our negative deeds. Through the spiritual cleansing power of water, we wash our hands and destroy all forms of negativity.

There is an extra ו in the word *Urchatz*. This extra ו [*Vav*] indicates the importance of physically washing our hands as opposed to just meditating on them. Each time we draw Light, we must manifest it through a physical action. Good thoughts are not enough. There must be a follow-through deed. As the saying goes, actions speak louder than words. The act of washing hands destroys the negative forces. Merely thinking will never achieve results.

### STAGE THREE: KARPAS

כַּרְפַּס

We can rearrange the letters of the word *Karpas* as follows: ס פרך
This spells the phrase *Samech Perach* – "the hard work of the 600,000 people in Egypt."

Traditionally, we are told that the slavery and hard work that the Israelites endured involved whips, chains, and the dreaded Pharaoh, who kept the Israelites enslaved in Egypt. The Torah states, however, that the Israelites had it pretty good in Egypt. They kept begging Moses to take them back to Egypt every time things got a little rough in the desert during their Exodus.

The great Kabbalist the Ari explains that the exile was not physical in nature. It was a spiritual exile. The story of Passover is about freedom from the self and inner denial.

As long as they were slaves in Egypt, the Israelites were not accountable or responsible for their lives. They were victims. If any chaos fell upon them, they did not have to look in the mirror and accept blame. It's much easier to be a victim (slave) than it is to accept responsibility for life's problems.

This victim mindset was the real slavery that was occurring in Egypt. The exile of the Israelites led to genuine freedom and control over the cosmos, but with freedom and control there comes responsibility – and that was an uncomfortable prospect for the Israelites. This is the spiritual significance behind the Israelites' constant complaints and desires to return to Egypt. They were trying to shun the responsibility that was about to be thrust upon them. It was much easier for them to be enslaved by their ego and be victims of circumstance while their reactive nature laid all the blame for their chaos on people and events "out of their control."

But the reality is this: No event is out of our control. And each of us has the same problem. Our reactive nature blinds us to the freedom that is possible for us. Ignorance is bliss, as the saying goes. It's much easier to be a slave to ignorance and remain a victim than it is to be freed from this bondage and take on the heavy responsibility that goes with being masters of our destiny. All of a sudden, we have to look in the mirror and blame ourselves for every ounce of chaos and hardship that befalls us. But a moment after we accept this responsibility, we have the power of freedom and control over the cosmos in the palm of our hand.

Through the *Karpas*, we gain the ability to become the masters of our destiny. We gain the strength to accept the spiritual truth that only we are responsible for our good fortune and our misfortune.

We might ask, "How can a piece of parsley possibly give us this enormous power of freedom?" Just as a microscopic atom contains enough raw energy to vaporize an entire city, the spiritual energy of the parsley, on this one night, has the power to vaporize our reactive nature. The energy is contained in the Hebrew letters that compose the word *parsley*. Eating the parsley is simply the physical action required to bring this energy into manifestation.

We take a piece of celery/parsley, dip it in salt water, and bless it as follows:

בָּרוּךְ אַתָּה יְהֹוָאהּהּיִאהּהּיִיִיּי אֱלֹהֵינוּ יּלּהּ מֶלֶךְ הָעוֹלָם

בּוֹרֵא פְּרִי הָאֲדָמָה:

*Blessed are You, Hashem, our God, King of the universe, Who creates the fruit of the earth.*

### STAGE FOUR: YACHATZ

This word means "to split." We take the physical *Matzah* and split it in two. One is the *Afikoman*. The other remains on the Seder plate. The lesson for us is to realize that half of

our nature is negative. The other half is positive. At any given point, we are fifty-fifty. A positive action swings us over to positive. Likewise, a negative action pulls the other half over to the negative.

The *Afikoman* is considered the positive half. It is always bigger than the other to show us that if we perform a positive action, we can swing everything over to the positive side. We are never to believe that the Satan and our reactive side are stronger. This particular stage helps us defeat the Satan.

Another lesson concerns the idea of separating the soul consciousness from the body consciousness. We can either choose to connect to the essence of our soul or to the desires of the body in our day-to-day life.

A human being has three levels of energy:

1. Nshamah   – the soul            (top level)
2. Ruach     – the spirit          (middle level)
3. Nefesh    – the physical body (lower level)

The natural tendency of the physical body is to desire and receive for the self alone. All our negative traits and impure attributes are rooted in the body. Our soul is imbued with only positive traits, including a constant urge to share.

The decisions we make in life and the actions we carry out should always be rooted in the middle level of spirit – the Ruach. In the realm of spirit, we have the free will to choose which side we want to connect ourselves to – the lower level of the body or the top level of the soul.

The natural reactive instinct is to always choose the body, thinking only about ourselves. The alternative is to shut down the reactive instinct of the body and become proactive. We can exercise our free will[7] and choose to connect to the top level, our soul, where we begin to think about others first. We make an effort to start learning how to share and care about the people around us. Not because it is morally correct, but because sharing is the way to generate lasting spiritual Light in our lives.

### SPLITTING THE *MATZAH*

The concept of connecting to the top level of the soul correlates to the top *Matzah*. The middle Matzah embodies the level of spirit, while the bottom *Matzah* signifies the body.[8]

We are now going to use these three instruments called matzah to help us spiritually cleanse ourselves and reprogram our lives. The next instruction given to us by the ancient Kabbalists involves splitting the middle *Matzah*. This split signifies the dividing and separating of good and evil. This gives us the ability to recognize both our good

---

7. The only time we become true human beings, rising above the level of the animal kingdom, is when we exercise the greatest gift the Creator gave us—free will. Contrary to most philosophical teachings, free will is the most difficult attribute to both understand and master. Ninety-nine percent of the time, we never use our free will. We live our lives in a purely robotic manner, blindly following every whim and desire of the body. We are enslaved to the reactive will of our egos. Free will occurs only when we choose *not* to react to a given external event. That's it. Everything else in life is merely a prerecorded movie with scenes and characters designed to trigger reactions within us. The Satan attempts to feed us lines of dialogue and creates scenes that will feed and nourish our egos. Our goal is to get out of the Satan's movie and into a starring role in the movie produced by the Creator.

8. This three-level structure of the Matzot is not symbolic. We are not speaking in metaphorical terms. Each Matzah is a unique device and mechanism for connecting to the three levels of our very soul and essence. Just as sand in the ground is used to make the most powerful microchips on the planet, wheat in the fields is used to make the most powerful spiritual microchips—the Matzah.

tendencies and our negative tendencies. When we make the split, it is important to break the *Matzah* into one large piece and one smaller piece. The bigger half of the split *Matzah* is known as the *Afikoman*.

### The *Afikoman*

The bigger half of the split *Matzah* is known as the *Afikoman*. There is a tradition of hiding the *Afikoman* somewhere in the room, then having all the children look for it after the meal. The smaller half of the *Matzah* remains with us. In Kabbalah, tradition is not a reason, in and of itself, for performing any rite or ritual. There must be a practical benefit to our life. Understanding the spiritual significance behind this action gives us insight into human nature and helps us become more spiritually minded and happier people.

The bigger piece of *Matzah* (*Afikoman*) represents physical, material pleasure. The smaller piece represents spiritual fulfillment (and for that reason it is smaller).

In the early years of life, a child is predominantly made up of desire. When a baby is born, he wants material pleasure for himself alone – eating, sleeping, playing with toys. There is no concept of sharing or spirituality within his nature. The child instinctively knows that his cries will get him everything he desires. As the baby grows older, we hope his or her desires for the physical world decrease while the desires for spiritual possessions gradually expand. The Seder meal is a microcosm of this spiritual development.

We eat the bigger piece of *Matzah* – signifying our physical world – *after* the Seder, since our desire to eat is no longer controlling us. We've finished our meal, and hopefully, through the tools of the Seder, we have purified our soul and our *desire to receive for the self alone*. We've resisted eating the bigger piece at the beginning, when our appetite was at its highest level. Now we partake of the physical world (signified by eating the large *Matzah*) without any *desire to receive* controlling us. This simple but spiritually powerful action imbues us with the inner strength to control all our self-indulgent desires through the entire year.

Another spiritual secret concerning the hiding of the *Afikoman* concerns positive actions, good deeds, and the manner in which we should conduct our lives. All of our positive actions, including charity, should be hidden and concealed.[9] A prayer recited on Rosh Hashanah says that God remembers all that is forgotten. The Kabbalists explain that God remembers only the good actions and values and counts only the positive deeds that people forgot.[10] This connection of *Yachatz* helps us forget about our past positive deeds, which oftentimes make us spiritually complacent, and focuses us on the next round of positive actions that we can still achieve today and tomorrow.

---

9. Charity, according to Kabbalah, is not dependent upon how much one gives but rather how much one gives of himself, relative to his personal situation. In other words, charity that is given for tax purposes, plaques on a wall, names on a building, or honorary dinners are worthless in the spiritual realm. Many people do positive actions out of concern for what other people will say about them. Real charity is when we go outside of our comfort zone and there is a true element of sacrifice. Second, a charitable action must be concealed without any reward or recognition for the ego. The highest form of charity is when a person gives without ever knowing to whom he gave and the recipient does not know who gave to him. These kinds of acts bring genuine blessing to the giver.

10. Instead of patting ourselves on the back, constantly congratulating ourselves over our acts of charity, we must forget about them and move on to the next positive action. Spiritual growth is a constant climb upward to the next level. Standing still or becoming spiritually complacent is akin to standing on a downward escalator. If we do not move forward but remain in one place, we fall backwards. We must continually climb the downward escalator, our ego.

*Magid* is a derivative of the Hebrew word for "speaking" and "to say," signifying the power of speech. We are using the power of speech when we recite these *Hagaddah* stories. The act of speaking throughout this section connects us to the Thirteen Attributes[11] of the Creator. This connection imbues us with the energy force of miracles. Moses used this ancient Kabbalistic meditation to jump-start all the miracles[12] that were necessary to release the Israelites from Egypt.[13]

## Revealing the Matzas and the Raising of the Seder Plate

The Seder plate represents the *Sfirah* of Malchut,[14] our physical world. The level of Malchut also represents God's presence in this world, known by the code term *Shechinah*.

The Shechinah materializes in this world by dwelling in the Temple in Jerusalem. From this unique location, it transmits God's Light to the entire world. Without the physical temple, the Shechinah has no place to reveal itself. During the many exiles of the Israelites,[15] including the expulsion from Spain in 1492 and the Holocaust in 1942, the Shechinah has also been in exile. For this reason, we lack the Shechinah's power of protection. As we raise the Seder plate, we are helping to raise ourselves and the Shechinah out of exile.[16]

---

11. The thirteen Attributes are thirteen virtues or properties that reflect thirteen aspects of our relationship with the Creator. These 13 Attributes are how we interact with God in our daily lives, whether we know it or not. They work like a mirror. When we look into a mirror and smile, the image smiles back. When we look into a mirror and curse, the image curses back. If we perform a negative action in our world, the mirror reflects negative energy at us. There are Thirteen Attributes that have these reflecting properties within us. As we attempt to transform our reactive nature to proactive, this feedback directs, guides, and corrects us. The number 13 also represents one above the twelve signs of the zodiac. The twelve signs control our instinctive, reactive nature. The number thirteen gives us control over the twelve signs, which, in essence, gives us control over our behavior.
12. We can use this ancient energy associated with miracles to generate miracles in our own life. We often find it difficult to break free of negative and harmful habits. Likewise, we find that positive habits are almost impossible to come by. The energy of miracles can give us the additional strength we need to alter our lives permanently so that negative habits and destructive behavior are no longer running our life.
13. *Egypt* is a code word for our ego and selfish *desire to receive for the oneself alone*. All of us are held in bondage by our reactive nature. It is our ego—the Satan—who is our true taskmaster. The Satan is so good at his job, the majority of us don't even realize that we are in bondage.
14. The 10 Sfirot are 10 dimensions that separate our physical world from the realm of the Endless World, where God's Light blazes with infinite illumination. See ten Sfirot appendix and explanation.
15. Exile of the Israelites is caused by insensitivity, intolerance, and jealousy between one Jew and another. Rav Berg teaches us that there are two kinds of jealousy, one of which is far more dangerous and is the cause of the exile. The first jealousy is when someone envies the possessions of another. He might be motivated to acquire similar possessions, but the jealous person is not wishing any kind of ill-will toward the other person. The second kind of jealousy, which, incidentally, both the Talmud and Kabbalah claim is exclusive to the nature of the Israelites, is when a person has the *same* personal effects and belongings as his neighbor, but the jealous person still envies and begrudges the other person for having the exact same items as himself. In other words, no one else should have anything, but himself. This kind of ill-will and jealousy toward others is what generates tremendous negative forces that eventually strike back at the Israel nation.
16. All our actions, including the raising of the plate, are not symbolic; they are actual tools and keys that activate powerful metaphysical forces that can dramatically alter our lives for the better. Having

Another way to empower this action is to feel the pain of the Shechinah. One reason the Shechinah is not in its correct space – the temple – is because we are not in the right head space.[17] We must feel the pain of the Shechinah since it is our negative actions that are the cause behind its exile in the first place.

After we uncover the *Matzot*, and raised the Seder plate, we say:

### L'SHEM YICHUD

L'shem Yichud acts as a spark plug that activates our desire to connect to spiritual energy. It also serves as a preparation process, readying us for the tremendous forces streaming into our world.

לְשֵׁם יְחוּד קֻדְשָׁא בְּרִיךְ הוּא וּשְׁכִינְתֵּיה בִּדְחִילוּ וּרְחִימוּ

וּרְחִימוּ וּדְחִילוּ לְיַחֲדָא שֵׁם יוּד קֵי בְּוָאו קֵי בְּיִחוּדָא שְׁלִים

יהוה בְּשֵׁם כָּל יִשְׂרָאֵל, הֲרֵינִי מוּכָן וּמְזוּמָן לְקַיֵּם הַמִּצְוָה

לְסַפֵּר בִּיצִיאַת מִצְרַיִם מצר, וִיהִי נֹעַם אֲדֹנָי אֱלֹהֵינוּ יהו עָלֵינוּ

וּמַעֲשֵׂה יָדֵינוּ כּוֹנְנָה עָלֵינוּ וּמַעֲשֵׂה יָדֵינוּ כּוֹנְנֵהוּ:

*For the sake of unifying The Holy One, blessed be It, and Its Shechinah, with fear and mercy, and with mercy and fear, to unify the name of Yud Key with Vav Key completely, in the name of all Israel, I am ready and willing to apply the connection of telling about the Exodus from Egypt, and may the pleasantness of Hashem, our God, be upon us, and establish the action of our hands upon us and establish the action of our hands.*

### HA LACHMA ANYA

*This is the bread that we ate in Egypt.* The purpose of reciting this verse is to understand and internalize the following idea: *Bread* is a code word[18] and an instrument that connects to our ego and reactive nature. Bondage refers to our slavery to our ego and selfish desires. *Matzah* is best described as bread without ego. God cannot give us 100-percent fulfillment when we are into our own ego. We came to this physical to rid ourselves of our selfish desires.

---

*certainty* in the spiritual power of the ritual is what sets these metaphysical forces into action. In other words, when we believe, we achieve.

17. Throughout history, the people have been ignorant of these spiritual explanations behind the rites and rituals of Passover. Consequently, the proper meditation and intent was lacking when they were carried out. This is why pain and suffering has been the trademark of the Israelites for centuries. Each of us should appreciate that we now have Kabbalah to at least explain the actions and the spiritual forces behind them.

18. Bread is an all-powerful tool in Kabbalah. Bread is a direct link to our internal reactive nature and ego. Just as bread has the power to expand and rise, our ego has the ability to expand and motivate us to rise to great heights in the material world. *Matzah* is like bread without ego, bread that has had its reactive nature shut down. By tasting the *Matzah*, with the proper meditation and intent, we receive the power to shut down our ego so that we can free ourselves from the slavery of reactive behavior and rise to great spiritual heights in our life.

Reciting this verse awakens us to all our personal negative traits that we specifically came to correct in this lifetime. *This is the Bread we ate in Egypt* can be translated into spiritual terms to mean "These are our negative traits [Bread] that enslave us in our day-to-day lives [Egypt]."

## This is the Bread

The word *Anya* means "poor." It is also translated to mean "the bread of the poor man." The Zohar says that the only prayers that are accepted into Heaven are those of the poor. Does that exclude the rich from having their prayers answered? Absolutely not. If a rich man realizes that he could lose all his wealth in a moment, and that he is not the architect of his own success, he fits the spiritual description of a poor man. In other words, we must factor the unlimited influence of the Light into the equation of our financial success. We must recognize that the Light is the source of all good fortune and that the Satan will manipulate our ego to make us believe that we are the geniuses behind our success.

The numerical value of the word *Ha Lachma Anya* equals the value of the Hebrew word *Kav Yamin*, which means "Right Column."[19] Right Column signifies pure sharing and unconditional caring. There is no hidden agenda of wanting something in return. The secret to liberating ourselves from bondage is to arouse this kind of no-strings-attached caring and sharing for others. We must also eradicate any and all judgment we might have for our friends and our enemies.

The *Ha* in *Ha Lachma* represents the underlined Hebrew letter *Hei* (ה) from the יהוה, a sequence of Hebrew letters that transmit the Light of God. The Hebrew letter ה correlates to the vessel of humanity as we exist in this physical world. This is also known as Malchut.[20] Malchut represents both humanity and the moon for the following reason: The moon has no light of its own. All of the moon's light is derived from the sun. Humanity also has no spiritual Light of its own. Our Light is derived from the Creator through our positive actions and transformation of character.

Kabbalah teaches us that King David is the personification of Malchut. When King David was born into our world, he came with no Light of his own. He was destined to die at birth. Adam foresaw this situation, however, and gave seventy years of his own life so that King David could live. Thus, instead of living 1,000 years, we learn that Adam lived 930 years.

הָא לַחְמָא עַנְיָא דִּי אֲכָלוּ אַבְהָתָנָא בְּאַרְעָא דְמִצְרָיִם מצר־

כָּל יּ־ דִּכְפִין יֵיתֵי וְיֵיכוֹל. כָּל יּ־ דִּצְרִיךְ יֵיתֵי וְיִפְסַח.

*This is the poor bread that our forefathers ate in the land of Egypt. Let all the hungry people come and eat. Let all the needy come and celebrate the Passover.*

---

19. There are three forces built into the universe—the force of sharing (Right Column), the force of receiving (Left Column), and the force of balance (Central Column). These three forces exist both in the physical and spiritual worlds. Physically, they represent the proton (Right Column), the electron (Left Column), and the neutron (Central Column). These three subatomic particles are the building blocks of the atom. Spiritually, they represent our *desire to share* (Right Column), our *desire to receive* (Left Column), and our free will to balance these two desires (Central Column). We need to balance these three forces for the following reasons: A person who constantly shares, without any aspect of receiving or replenishment, will eventually become depleted and empty. A person, who constantly receives, without any sharing, will become overloaded with energy and short-circuit. Our purpose in this world is to nullify our selfish *desire to receive for the self alone* and transform it into a *desire to receive for the sake of sharing*. By constantly sharing and receiving, we strike a perfect balance.

20. See appendix on the Ten Sfirot.

הָשַׁתָּא הָכָא לְשָׁנָה הַבָּאָה בְּאַרְעָא דְיִשְׂרָאֵל. הָשַׁתָּא

עַבְדֵי לְשָׁנָה הַבָּאָה בְּנֵי חֹורִין:

*This year, over here – next year, in the land of Israel. This year, slaves – next year, free.*

### THE SECOND CUP OF WINE – BRIAH

There are four cups of wine poured during the course of the Seder. These cups signify and connect us to the four-letter name of God, the Tetragrammaton[21] – and four Upper Worlds in our spiritual atmosphere. The names of these worlds are Atzilut, Briah, Yetzirah, Asiyah.

### MA NISHTANAH – THE FOUR QUESTIONS

The are four questions dealing with why Passover is different from all other nights. The traditional and literal answer given in the *Hagaddah* is: *we were slaves in Egypt.*

On the surface, this response does not answer the question in a manner that has direct relevance to our lives today. Kabbalah explains that there is a deeper question being raised by the *Hagaddah*: Why did the sages prescribe the actions of the Passover Seder on this very night? According to the Hebrew calendar, tonight, and only tonight, there's a unique window of opportunity in the cosmos. The prison-cell door and leg irons are suddenly unlocked. We have the chance to escape and flee the prison of our ego. This opening was created some 3,000 years ago when the Israelites were freed from slavery on this very same date. Because energy never dissipates, the energy of freedom returns every year on this night. We can capture this energy through the methodology of Kabbalah and the actions of the Seder. If we behave spiritually, the way we did in Egypt many centuries ago, we can free ourselves from all the slavery we're experiencing today.[22] If we behave the same way as we do on all other nights of the year, this freedom cannot be accomplished. We must act differently.[23] The actions that we are performing during the Seder possess the same power and spiritual energy that the Israelites aroused in Egypt. All we have to do is mirror those moves to capture the same force of freedom.

Whatever kind of year we had previous, whatever level we have attained spiritually, we are automatically on a higher level during Passover. For example, the great Kabbalist Rabbi Yitzchak Luria was already on a high level. His Passover was therefore on an even higher level than he was on all other nights. Here's the advantage for us: One of the benefits of thinking to be completely unified as one, with everyone at our Seder, is that we

---

21. The Tetragrammaton is a powerful combination of Hebrew letters that literally transmits the spiritual forces of the Upper World into our physical existence. The four letters of the Tetragrammaton are: יהוה.

22. All of us are enslaved to our egos and our material existence. We are held prisoner, captives to our careers, jobs, relationships, fears, and anxieties. Or we are held in bondage, slaves to other people's perceptions of us. We are incarcerated by our own desperate need for other people's acceptance. Tonight, we can break free from all these strangleholds. The freedom that occurred in Egypt some 3,300 years ago was for one purpose—to create a reservoir of energy for all future generations so that we could access the power of freedom in our personal lives.

23. During and after the Seder, and especially when we get back into the real world, we cannot be the same person we were the year before. We must make an effort to become more tolerant and compassionate. Not because it is morally correct behavior, but because this kind of behavior, and the freedom it brings, is what will give us genuine and lasting fulfillment.

automatically attain the highest level of the person in the room, regardless of our own level. Therefore, it's in our own interest to surround ourselves with the most positive spiritual people possible on this one night of the year.

While pouring the second cup, the child asks:

מַה מ״ה נִּשְׁתַּנָּה הַלַּיְלָה והו הַזֶּה מלה מִכָּל הַלֵּילוֹת.

שֶׁבְּכָל לכב הַלֵּילוֹת אָנוּ אוֹכְלִין חָמֵץ וּמַצָּה. הַלַּיְלָה מלה
הַזֶּה והו כֻּלּוֹ מַצָּה:

שֶׁבְּכָל לכב הַלֵּילוֹת אָנוּ אוֹכְלִין שְׁאָר יְרָקוֹת. הַלַּיְלָה מלה
הַזֶּה והו כֻּלּוֹ מָרוֹר:

שֶׁבְּכָל לכב הַלֵּילוֹת אֵין אָנוּ מַטְבִּילִין אֲפִילוּ פַּעַם מנק אֶחָת.
הַלַּיְלָה מלה הַזֶּה והו שְׁתֵּי פְּעָמִים:

שֶׁבְּכָל לכב הַלֵּילוֹת אָנוּ אוֹכְלִין בֵּין יוֹשְׁבִין וּבֵין מְסֻבִּין.
הַלַּיְלָה מלה הַזֶּה והו כֻּלָּנוּ מְסֻבִּין:

*What differentiates this night from all other nights? All other nights we may eat both bread and Matzah. Tonight is all Matzah. All other nights we may eat all sorts of vegetables. Tonight is all horseradish. All other nights we do not dip even once. Tonight (we dip) twice. All other nights we may eat either sitting (or reclining) or partying (on cushioned chairs). Tonight all of us are reclining.*

## AVADIM HA'YINU
### We were slaves in Egypt and God took us out of bondage.

This verse is not just referring to our ancestors back in ancient Egypt. It's a direct reference to us. Further, this verse is teaching us that the only way a person can gain real freedom is through the power of Pesach.

It's interesting to note the observations of 16th-century Kabbalist Rabbi Yitzzchak Luria: The Ari explained that only *after* the Israelites attained genuine spiritual freedom were they able to receive the revelation on Mount Sinai and the state of immortality that revelation produced.[24] The power of Pesach was the prerequisite for the Light of immortality being revealed on Sinai. In practical terms, we must free ourselves from the bondage of our reactive nature to attain the greatest of all rewards – the complete

---

24. How many of us would be willing to endure a little Egypt, a little discomfort, to attain true immortality? We must be willing to free ourselves from the bondage of our ego, which can be very painful on our pride, to attain lasting fulfillment in life.

revelation of the Light in our physical world – the Mashiach.[25]

We reveal the *Matzot* and say:

עֲבָדִים הָיִינוּ לְפַרְעֹה בְּמִצְרָיִם מצר- וַיּוֹצִיאֵנוּ יְהֹוָֽאֲדֹנֵיאהדונהי

אֱלֹהֵינוּ ילה- מִשָּׁם בְּיָד חֲזָקָה וּבִזְרֹעַ נְטוּיָה וְאִלּוּ לֹא הוֹצִיא

הַקָּדוֹשׁ בָּרוּךְ הוּא אֶת אֲבוֹתֵינוּ מִמִּצְרַיִם מצר הֲרֵי אָנוּ

וּבָנֵינוּ וּבְנֵי בָנֵינוּ מְשֻׁעְבָּדִים הָיִינוּ לְפַרְעֹה בְּמִצְרָיִם מצר-

וַאֲפִילוּ כֻּלָּנוּ חֲכָמִים כֻּלָּנוּ נְבוֹנִים כֻּלָּנוּ זְקֵנִים כֻּלָּנוּ יוֹדְעִים

אֶת הַתּוֹרָה מִצְוָה עָלֵינוּ לְסַפֵּר בִּיצִיאַת מִצְרָיִם מצר-. וְכָל

הַמַּרְבֶּה לְסַפֵּר בִּיצִיאַת מִצְרָיִם מצר- הֲרֵי זֶה מְשֻׁבָּח:

*We were enslaved to Pharaoh in Egypt. Then Hashem, our God, took us out from there with a mighty hand and an outstretched arm. Had not The Holy One, blessed be It, taken our fathers out from Egypt, then we, our children, and our grandchildren would have remained enslaved to Pharaoh in Egypt. Even if we were all wise, understanding, experienced, and knowledgeable about the Torah, we would still need to make the connection through telling about the Exodus from Egypt. The more one tells about the Exodus, the better.*

### The Story of the Five Sages[26]

One Seder night, some 2,000 years ago, five great sages were sitting in the city of Bnei Brak in Israel having a lengthy discourse on the Exodus from Egypt. Suddenly, their students came in to tell them that the morning prayers had arrived. The sages had completely lost track of time, completely absorbed in the wonderment of the story. The Kabbalists tell us that when we absorb ourselves in spiritual work, forgetting all about the limitations of time, space, and motion, God will remove all the limitations that are holding us back. King David said, "God is our shadow." If we remain enslaved to the physical constraints of time, space, and motion, these limitations will be reflected back to us. If we

---

25. Kabbalistically, the Mashiach is not someone who is coming to save us, but rather the age of Mashiach will occur when we free ourselves from our self-centered desires of the ego that attempt to motivate us all day long. Self-freedom is the necessary step before *to* the reality of immortality and total happiness can become manifest.

26. Every story in the Hagaddah is actually a code that conceals hidden wisdom. There is law at work in Kabbalah: To reveal, you must first conceal. A seed must be buried and concealed in the ground before a tree and fruit can be revealed. A baby is first concealed in the womb of its mother before a child can be revealed in our world. The secret wisdom of life must first be concealed inside a story before the lesson can be revealed and absorbed by the student of Kabbalah. For that reason, many stories, when taken literally, seem oddly out of touch with our present-day life. We must probe beyond the surface level of a story to expose the message and meaning concealed inside. Every word has a numerical value, each sentence a simple translation, and other codes that serve to enshroud the spiritual significance in a cloak of simplicity and apparent irrelevance.

just let go, relinquish control, and stop worrying about the constraints of our physical world in order to embrace more spiritual work, the Light will remove all the friction, obstacles, and barriers associated with time, space, and motion.

Another lesson from this simple story is that the *Hagaddah* has devoted valuable space to include the appearance of the students, giving them equal billing to the great holy sages. The lesson is that we can all learn from everyone and anyone. The Talmud makes the statement, "Who is a smart person? The one who learns from every person!" Everybody in this world is our teacher – the positive people and the negative people. Everything and everybody that we come into contact with is there to teach us something about our own character and area of correction.

מַעֲשֶׂה בְּרַבִּי אֱלִיעֶזֶר וְרַבִּי יְהוֹשֻׁעַ וְרַבִּי אֶלְעָזָר בֶּן עֲזַרְיָה
וְרַבִּי עֲקִיבָא וְרַבִּי טַרְפוֹן שֶׁהָיוּ מְסֻבִּין בִּבְנֵי בְרַק וְהָיוּ
מְסַפְּרִים בִּיצִיאַת מִצְרַיִם מצר־ כָּל יל־ אוֹתוֹ הַלַּיְלָה מלה־ עַד
שֶׁבָּאוּ תַלְמִידֵיהֶם וְאָמְרוּ לָהֶם רַבּוֹתֵינוּ הִגִּיעַ זְמַן קְרִיאַת
שְׁמַע שֶׁל שַׁחֲרִית:

*Once upon a time, Rabbi Eliezer, Rabbi Yehoshua, Rabbi El'azar ben Azaryah, Rabbi Akiva, and Rabbi Tarfon were reclining (at the Seder) in Bnei Brak, telling about the Exodus all that night, until their students came and said to them: "Our teachers, it is time to read the morning Sh'ma."*

### AMAR RABBI ELAZAR

This story tells of Rabbi Elazar, who was 18 years old when he was asked to become the leader of the nation. He had a great fear that no one would respect him because of his youth, so God made him look 70 years old. The spiritual lesson behind the literal story concerns the power of mind over matter. What we believe, we will achieve. Positive or negative.

There is a discourse by Rabbi Elazar that concerns the telling of the Exodus story only at night. Once again, the literal story conceals a spiritual code. *Daylight* refers to positive times when things are going extremely well for us. The Light of the Creator is shining brightly in our eyes. *Night* refers to those moments of darkness when we are up to our neck in chaos and obstacles. Rabbi Elazar is teaching us that we must demonstrate an equal amount of certainty and conviction in the Light of the Creator when times are difficult and the doubts try to consume us as we do when things are going well and we experience those mystical moments where we can feel God's presence in our life.

אָמַר רַבִּי אֶלְעָזָר בֶּן עֲזַרְיָה הֲרֵי אֲנִי אני כְּבֶן שִׁבְעִים שָׁנָה

*Said Rabbi Elazar ben Azaryah: "I am like a seventy year-old man,*

וְלֹא זָכִיתִי שֶׁתֵּאָמֵר יְצִיאַת מִצְרַיִם מצר- בַּלֵּילוֹת עַד

שֶׁדְּרָשָׁהּ בֶּן זוֹמָא, שֶׁנֶּאֱמַר, לְמַעַן תִּזְכֹּר אֶת יוֹם גגד, זן

צֵאתְךָ מֵאֶרֶץ מִצְרַיִם מצר- כֹּל יל- יְמֵי חַיֶּיךָ: יְמֵי חַיֶּיךָ

הַיָּמִים גג- כֹּל יל- יְמֵי חַיֶּיךָ הַלֵּילוֹת. וַחֲכָמִים אוֹמְרִים יְמֵי

חַיֶּיךָ הָעוֹלָם הַזֶּה הה- כֹּל יל- יְמֵי חַיֶּיךָ לְהָבִיא לִימוֹת הַמָּשִׁיחַ:

*And yet was never privileged to have the Exodus from Egypt mentioned at nights, until Ben Zoma expounded it: 'in order that you remember the day you left Egypt all the days of your life.' The days of your life' refers to the days alone; while 'all the days…' refers also to the nights. And the sages say that 'the days of your life' refers to this world alone, while 'all the days…' refers also to bring us to the time of Messiah.*

### BARUCH HAMAKOM
#### Blessed is God who gave us the Torah
We are grateful for the Torah because before its revelation, we did not know how to connect to the Creator in a practical way. It is similar to having a telephone but not having the correct phone number to dial for help.[27]

There is a famous story about the great sage Hillel that reveals the concept of "love thy neighbor as thyself"[28] Even this well-known concept was unknown until the revelation of the Torah. The appreciation of the Torah is for our opportunity to penetrate to its inner spiritual essence, capturing any amount of energy we desire to bring meaning and fulfillment to our lives.

בָּרוּךְ הַמָּקוֹם בָּרוּךְ הוּא בָּרוּךְ שֶׁנָּתַן תּוֹרָה לְעַמּוֹ

יִשְׂרָאֵל. בָּרוּךְ הוּא.

*Blessed is the Omnipresent, blessed is He. Blessed is the One Who gave the Torah to His people, Israel, blessed is He."*

There are four paths we can use when connecting to God:

כְּנֶגֶד זן, מזבוח אַרְבָּעָה בָנִים דִּבְּרָה תוֹרָה:

*The Torah speaks about four sons:*

---

27. The sequence of letters and words in the Torah are the correct phone number to dial God. The scroll can be likened to the actual telephone, while the parchment works like a long-distance carrier.

28. A convert once came to Hillel and asked the great sage to explain all the sublime secrets and magnificent mysteries of the Torah in the short time it takes to remain balanced on one leg. Hillel gave careful consideration to this request. He then replied to the student, "Love thy neighbor as thyself. All the rest is commentary. Now, go and learn."

אֶחָד אהבה וָכָם׃ וְאֶחָד אהבה רָשָׁע? וְאֶחָד אהבה תָּם׃

וְאֶחָד אהבה שֶׁאֵינוֹ יוֹדֵעַ לִשְׁאוֹל:

*A wise one, a wicked one, a simple one, and one who does not know enough to raise a question.*

### THE WISE ONE

A wise person asks, "Why are we performing all these rites and rituals on Passover? Are they merely physical actions for the sake of tradition and remembrance?" As explained in the section on the *Afikoman*, only when we conquer our *desire to receive* and attain real freedom from it do we eat the *Afikoman*. That explanation is deeper spiritual significance behind the ritual associated with the *Afikoman*.

We classify this person as wise by virtue of his desire to seek the spiritual truth that lies beyond the literal telling of the story, beyond the tradition. A person can attain a high spiritual level only if he continually probes and questions beyond the physical level of reality. He journeys into the concealed and hidden truths.

וָכָם מ״ה מָה הוּא אוֹמֵר׃ מָה מ״ה הָעֵדוֹת וְהַחֻקִּים

וְהַמִּשְׁפָּטִים אֲשֶׁר צִוָּה יְהֹוָֹה אֲדֹהִיאהדונהי אֱלֹהֵינוּ יכֹה אֶתְכֶם׃

וְאַף אַתָּה אֱמוֹר לוֹ כְּהִלְכוֹת הַפֶּסַח אֵין מַפְטִירִין אַחַר

הַפֶּסַח אֲפִיקוֹמָן:

*What does the wise son say? "What are the testimonies, decrees, and ordinances which Hashem, our God, has commanded you?" Therefore, explain to him according to the Pesach regulations – that one may not have dessert after the final taste of the Pesach offering.*

### THE WICKED ONE:

The wicked person tauntingly asks, "Why do you bother with all these rites and rituals?" It might appear to be a similar question to the one that the wise person asked. What's the difference between questions from the wise and wicked? The wicked comes from a negative place. His question is rooted in uncertainty and skepticism.

The hidden message in the wicked person's question is: "Nothing we do will work. Why should any of our actions change anything?"

A great Rabbi once said, "To questions there are answers, but to answers, there are no answers."

The wicked person already has the negative answer in his mind. He asks his questions rhetorically, as a way to put forth his negative opinions. He does not seek truth. He is not really asking a question but merely stating his pessimistic viewpoints to negatively influence others and advance his own agenda.

The underlying motivation behind the wicked person is his unwillingness to take responsibility for any of his negative actions. The Ari stated that the real exile in Egypt was the exile of the mind. The Egyptians literally programmed everyone to believe that there was no cause-and-effect principle at work in our universe. Everything was chance, randomness, and uncontrollable chaos. This perspective relieves us of any responsibility and accountability for our actions. The Egyptians would have magicians, who were versed in the occult arts,[29] perform random acts of black magic to prove the lack of order in our world. The real Exodus and freedom was our sudden awareness of the concealed order and universal laws at work in the universe.

The Israelites were so programmed, they did not even realize they were in slavery. For this same reason, a wicked person can never really leave Egypt because he doesn't even realize that he *is* in Egypt. The wicked is happy in his ways, ignorant to the truth that a far more fulfilling and happier life exists on a different path. Our lesson is this: We can gain real freedom and peace of mind in our lives by realizing and admitting that we are indeed slaves to our reactive nature. If we think everything is fine, we will never attain true freedom. The root of our own negativity is our inability to understand that whatever happens to us happens for a reason. Bad things occur to awaken us to our reactive ways.

We must make sure that when we ask questions concerning spiritual truths, we leave our preconceived notions and personal beliefs at the door. We must open ourselves up to objectively hear the spiritual viewpoint.

רָשָׁע מַה מ״ה הוּא אוֹמֵר. מַה מ״ה הָעֲבוֹדָה הַזֹּאת לָכֶם.

לָכֶם וְלֹא לוֹ. וּלְפִי שֶׁהוֹצִיא אֶת עַצְמוֹ מִן הַכְּלָל כָּפַר

בְּעִקָּר. וְאַף אַתָּה הַקְהֵה אֶת שִׁנָּיו וֶאֱמוֹר לוֹ. בַּעֲבוּר זֶה

עָשָׂה יְהֹוָ‏אֲדֹנָי‏אהדונהי לִי בְּצֵאתִי מִמִּצְרַיִם מצר. לִי וְלֹא לוֹ.

אִלּוּ הָיָה יהה שָׁם לֹא הָיָה יהה נִגְאָל:

*What does the wicked son say? "Of what purpose is this work to you?" He says "...to you," thereby excluding himself. By excluding himself from the congregation, he denies a basic principle. Therefore, blunt his teeth and tell him: "that is why Hashem did so for me, when I went out of Egypt." "For me" but not for him. Had he been there, he would not have been redeemed.*

### THE SIMPLE ONE:

The simple person asks, "Why did God have to kill all the Egyptians? Were we brought to this world to suffer? Why was there so much judgment on the Egyptians?" The traditional answer is that the Egyptians had to pay for all their negative actions. They brought the plagues upon themselves. Once again, the entire story of Exodus is a code that contains deeper spiritual significance. It is *we* who are the Egyptians. The Egyptians represent our own negative characteristics. When our lives our governed by our selfish impulses, we bring plagues of chaos onto ourselves.

---

29. The Egyptians knew how to connect to the Light through negative paths. For example, we can utilize the electrical current in our home to provide warmth and comfort to our family. Or we can use this current in destructive ways by sticking someone's finger into a wall socket. We have the free will to choose how to connect to the Light.

Another question often asked is, "Why must we perform the rituals of Passover every year? Why couldn't a great prophet like Moses accomplish the mission and bring peace forever?" Moses did not have the force of the people to further empower him. Therein lies the greatest advantage in our current age. Today we have the people, young and old, learning the secret wisdom of Kabbalah. When we achieve a critical mass, the final redemption, world peace and immortality will become the new reality.

תָּם מָה מ"ה הוּא אוֹמֵר. מַה מ"ה זֹּאת. וְאָמַרְתָּ אֵלָיו בְּחוֹזֶק

יָד הוֹצִיאָנוּ יְהֹוָאדניאהדונהי מִמִּצְרַיִם מצר מִבֵּית ב"פ ראה עֲבָדִים:

*What does the simple son say? "What is this?" Tell him: "With might did Hashem take us out of Egypt, from the house of bondage."*

### THE ONE WHO DOES NOT KNOW HOW TO ASK:

There are people who do not know how to ask the right questions. Oftentimes, we ourselves don't know what to do, what to ask, or where to look for answers.

The Zohar says, "Open me to the eye of a needle, and I will open to thee the Supernal Gates." Each one of us has a responsibility to help create the opening of the eye of a needle to all those who are lost and stuck in the mire of chaos. We have a responsibility to help family, friends, strangers, and everyone we come into contact with. We must activate the Light of sharing (not preach or coerce people) to help create an opening. That is really our opportunity to share.

וְשֶׁאֵינוֹ יוֹדֵעַ לִשְׁאוֹל אַתְּ פְּתַח לוֹ. שֶׁנֶּאֱמַר, וְהִגַּדְתָּ לְבִנְךָ

בַּיּוֹם גגד, זן הַהוּא לֵאמֹר בַּעֲבוּר זֶה עָשָׂה יְהֹוָאדניאהדונהי לִי

בְּצֵאתִי מִמִּצְרָיִם מצר:

*As for the one who is unable to ask, initiate the subject for him as stated: "And you shall tell your son on that day: 'Because of this, Hashem did so for me, when I went out of Egypt.'"*

### YACHOL MEROSH CHODESH

The Hagaddah asks why the Exodus did not begin on Rosh Chodesh, which is the seed of the entire month. Why are we connecting to the effect and not to the cause level, which always resides in the seed on Rosh Chodesh? The reason is that the month of Nissan, in which Passover appears, is one of the most powerful months of the year. Just as we require the Hebrew month of Elul to prepare us for the following month of Tishrei, in which Rosh Hashanah occurs,[30] we need the first 15 days of Nissan to prepare and build up our internal Vessel in order to receive the overwhelming energy of freedom.

The first twelve days of Nissan connect us to the twelve tribes of Israel, gathering them together, so to speak, in readiness for the Exodus. The connection to the twelve tribes

---

30. The month of Elul is supposed to be used as a preparation process for the next month, when Rosh Hashanah appears. Elul is a time of deep soul-searching, self-confession, and efforts to make amends to our friends and family for all the wrongdoing we've committed. The amount of spiritual garbage that we can uproot in Elul is the amount we can cleanse in Rosh Hashanah.

also gives us control over the twelve signs of the zodiac so that no negative astrological influences can disrupt or prevent our freedom from bondage.

What happens if we did not prepare ourselves during the first fifteen days because we were unaware of this concept until this moment? What if this is our first Kabbalistic Seder? Once again, the advantage of surrounding ourselves with positive spiritual people and making the effort to be unified with everyone is that we get to share in all the energy being aroused by all the participants. Those people who have taken all the necessary spiritual steps of preparation can share their effort and energy with us without diminishing the amount of energy they themselves receive.[31]

יָכוֹל מֵרֹאשׁ וֹּדֶשׁ ה״ב הויות, תַּלְמוּד לוֹמַר בַּיּוֹם גנד, ה הַהוּא.

אִי בַּיּוֹם גנד, ה הַהוּא, ה יָכוֹל מִבְּעוֹד יוֹם גנד ה, תַּלְמוּד לוֹמַר

בַּעֲבוּר זֶה. בַּעֲבוּר זֶה לֹא אָמַרְתִּי אֶלָּא בְּשָׁעָה שֶׁיֵּשׁ

מַצָּה וּמָרוֹר מֻנָּחִים לְפָנֶיךָ סמ״ב:

*One might think that the discussion of the Exodus commences with the first day of the month of Nissan, but the Torah says: "You shall tell your son on that day." The expression "on that day" may mean merely "during the daytime"; therefore, the Torah adds: "It is because of this that Hashem did so for me when I went out of Egypt." The pronoun "this" implies something tangible; thus, "you shall tell your son" applies only when Matzah and Maror lie before you – at the Seder.*

## MITCHILAH

This story contains the following phrase: *In the beginning our fathers were idol worshippers.* This is a direct reference to Avraham's father, Terach, who was the world's largest idol manufacturer. Avraham could have easily felt that because he was the son of an idol worshipper, he had no hope of transforming himself and discovering the truth about the Creator. Instead, Avraham realized that he could make his own mark in this world. Each of us can also overcome the inner forces that have kept us as idol worshippers.[32] It doesn't matter what happened yesterday or what our personal situation is, we can make a change of life if we decide to.

מִתְּחִלָּה עוֹבְדֵי עֲבוֹדָה זָרָה הָיוּ אֲבוֹתֵינוּ. וְעַכְשָׁיו קֵרְבָנוּ

הַמָּקוֹם לַעֲבוֹדָתוֹ.

*Originally our ancestors were idol worshipers, but now the Omnipresent has brought us near to its service.*

---

31. A person holding a single candle can share his flame with the candles of a thousand people without dimming the radiance of his own candlelight. This is the power of spiritual energy. The only prerequisite is to make an attempt of feeling love and unity for everyone around us.

32. Idol worshipping does not refer to manmade statues that we bow down to. An idol is defined as any material possessions that control our behavior and motivate us. If a material item determines our degree of happiness or sadness, then we have surrendered control. For some people, money is god. Others are disciples of their business or careers. Real freedom is about taking control over our own lives and emotions and generating happiness and emotional security from within.

שֶׁנֶּאֱמַר, וַיֹּאמֶר יְהוֹשֻׁעַ אֶל כָּל הָעָם כֹּה אָמַר

יְהֹוָה אֱלֹהֵי יִשְׂרָאֵל בְּעֵבֶר הַנָּהָר יָשְׁבוּ

אֲבוֹתֵיכֶם מֵעוֹלָם תֶּרַח אֲבִי אַבְרָהָם וַאֲבִי נָחוֹר

וַיַּעַבְדוּ אֱלֹהִים אֲחֵרִים: וָאֶקַּח אֶת אֲבִיכֶם אֶת אַבְרָהָם

מֵעֵבֶר הַנָּהָר וָאוֹלֵךְ אוֹתוֹ בְּכָל אֶרֶץ כְּנַעַן

וָאַרְבֶּה אֶת זַרְעוֹ וָאֶתֶּן לוֹ אֶת יִצְחָק, וָאֶתֵּן לְיִצְחָק

אֶת יַעֲקֹב וְאֶת עֵשָׂו וָאֶתֵּן לְעֵשָׂו אֶת הַר שֵׂעִיר לָרֶשֶׁת אוֹתוֹ, וְיַעֲקֹב וּבָנָיו יָרְדוּ מִצְרָיִם:

*As it is written, Joshua said to all the people: "So says Hashem, God of Israel: Your fathers always lived beyond the Euphrates River, Terach the father of Abraham and the father of Nachor, and they served other gods. Then I took your father Abraham from beyond the river and led him through all the land of Cna'an. I multiplied his offspring and gave him Isaac. To Isaac I gave Jacob and Esav. To Esav I gave Mount Se'ir to inherit, but Jacob and his children went down to Egypt."*

### BARUCH SHOMER
### Blessed is the one who keeps his promises to us.

This phrase is telling us that the force of the Creator never changes. It is only us who create the illusion of change.[33] One of the lessons for us is this: We should remain consistent on our spiritual path and not be concerned with other people's perceptions and opinions. We should constantly look for ways to share and stop our reactive impulses, regardless of the obstacles people throw our way. We must learn to never compromise our spiritual pursuits. We get the strength to remain consistent in our positive actions through this connection.

בָּרוּךְ שׁוֹמֵר הַבְטָחָתוֹ לְיִשְׂרָאֵל, בָּרוּךְ הוּא, שֶׁהַקָּדוֹשׁ

בָּרוּךְ הוּא וְחִשַּׁב אֶת הַקֵּץ לַעֲשׂוֹת. כְּמָה שֶׁאָמַר

לְאַבְרָהָם אָבִינוּ בִּבְרִית בֵּין הַבְּתָרִים.

*Blessed is that which keeps His pledge to Israel; blessed is He. For the Holy One, Blessed is He, calculated the end of bondage in order to do as He said to our father Abraham at the Covenant between the parts,*

---

33. A light bulb burning in a room shines consistently. If we cover the light with a blue gel, it radiates blue. A red gel changes the illumination to red. If we cover the light with a cloth, the light dims. If we cover the light bulb with a blanket, the light is completely concealed, leaving us in darkness. In all the above instances, the light itself never changed. The change was only from our perspective as a result of our own actions. The Light of the Creator is always there to share infinite fulfillment with us. It is up to us to remove the various coverings, filters, and curtains.

שֶׁנֶּאֱמַר, וַיֹּאמֶר לְאַבְרָם יָדֹעַ תֵּדַע כִּי גֵר יִהְיֶה ... זַרְעֲךָ
בְּאֶרֶץ לֹא לָהֶם וַעֲבָדוּם וְעִנּוּ אֹתָם אַרְבַּע מֵאוֹת שָׁנָה: וְגַם
אֶת הַגּוֹי אֲשֶׁר יַעֲבֹדוּ דָן אָנֹכִי וְאַחֲרֵי כֵן יֵצְאוּ בִּרְכֻשׁ גָּדוֹל:

*as it is stated: God said to Avraham, "know with certainty that your offspring will be aliens in a land not
their own; They will serve them and they will oppress them 400 years; but also upon the nation which they
shall serve will I execute judgment, and afterwards they shall leave with great possessions."*

### VHEE SHE'AMDAH

In every generation, God gives us the energy to free ourselves from bondage. If we should
ever believe that it is our own ego that provides freedom and fulfillment in our lives, we
can lose it all in a moment.

We now cover the *Matzah*, raise our cup of wine and say:

וְהִיא שֶׁעָמְדָה לַאֲבוֹתֵינוּ וְלָנוּ מוס אהבה שֶׁלֹּא אֶחָד בִּלְבָד
עָמַד עָלֵינוּ לְכַלּוֹתֵנוּ אֶלָּא שֶׁבְּכָל לכב דּוֹר וָדוֹר ריע עוֹמְדִים
עָלֵינוּ לְכַלּוֹתֵנוּ, וְהַקָּדוֹשׁ בָּרוּךְ הוּא מַצִּילֵנוּ מִיָּדָם:

*It is this that has stood by our fathers and us. For not only one has risen against us to annihilate us, but in every
generation they rise against us to annihilate us; and the Holy One, Blessed be He, rescues us from their hands.*

### TZE ULMAD

Yitzchak, the son of Avraham the Patriarch, had two sons, Esav the wicked and Ya'akov the
righteous. In the Torah story, we learn that a man named Lavan had two daughters,
Rachel and Leah. Rachel was destined to marry Ya'akov, while Leah was destined to marry
Esav. This is why, in the story, Leah is crying all the time. According to this marriage plan,
Rachel would then give birth to the twelve tribes. Lavan wanted to uproot everything. He
had Leah marry Ya'akov in the hopes that the twelve tribes would never be born and that
we'd never attain control over the twelve signs. We would remain slaves to the influences
of the twelve constellations.

We learn from this story that no matter how much an evil person schemes, Light always
overcomes darkness. Both Rachel and Leah ended up marrying Ya'akov. The twelve tribes
were born anyway. No matter how dark things appear to be, with God's help, we can
change it. Plans may change, but the outcome will always be positive. We also gain a
measure of control over the 12 signs simply be going through this particular stage.

We lower our cup of wine, reveal the Matzot say:

צֵא וּלְמַד

*Go and learn*

מַה מֶּ בִּקֵּשׁ לָבָן הָאֲרַמִּי לַעֲשׂוֹת לְיַעֲקֹב אָבִינוּ. שֶׁפַּרְעֹה

לֹא גָזַר אֶלָּא עַל הַזְּכָרִים וְלָבָן בִּקֵּשׁ לַעֲקוֹר אֶת הַכֹּל.

שֶׁנֶּאֱמַר: אֲרַמִּי אֹבֵד אָבִי וַיֵּרֶד ריי מִצְרַיְמָה מצר וַיָּגָר שָׁם

בִּמְתֵי מְעָט וַיְהִי שָׁם לְגוֹי גָּדוֹל עָצוּם וָרָב:

*what Lavan the Aramean attempted to do to our father Jacob. For Pharaoh decreed against only the males and Lavan attempted to uproot everything, as it is said: "An Aramean attempted to destroy my father. Then he descended to Egypt and sojourned there, with few people; and there he became a nation — great, mighty, and numerous.*

### VAYERED MITZRAYIMAH

The literal explanation tells us that Ya'akov traveled down into Egypt as a captive by virtue of an order issued by the word of God. The Kabbalist Rabbi Naftali Tzvi explains the spiritual meaning: The *word of God* is a code for the sacred words of the Torah. *Egypt* is a code for a person's own negativity. *Ya'akov* is a code signifying all the souls of Israel. Ya'akov went into "Egypt" to arouse the Light of the Creator so that he could defeat his own reactive nature. His purpose was to set up the spiritual framework that would pave the way for the revelation of the Torah on Mount Sinai some two and a half centuries later. If Ya'akov had not embarked on this perilous journey into the negativity, there would have been no way for the Torah to be revealed.

וַיֵּרֶד ריי מִצְרַיְמָה מצר אָנוּס עַל פִּי הַדִּבּוּר: וַיָּגָר שָׁם, מְלַמֵּד

שֶׁלֹּא יָרַד יַעֲקֹב אָבִינוּ לְהִשְׁתַּקֵּעַ בְּמִצְרַיִם מצר אֶלָּא לָגוּר

שָׁם. שֶׁנֶּאֱמַר, וַיֹּאמְרוּ אֶל פַּרְעֹה לָגוּר בָּאָרֶץ בָּאנוּ כִּי אֵין

מִרְעֶה לַצֹּאן אֲשֶׁר לַעֲבָדֶיךָ כִּי כָבֵד הָרָעָב בְּאֶרֶץ כְּנַעַן

וְעַתָּה יֵשְׁבוּ נָא עֲבָדֶיךָ בְּאֶרֶץ גֹּשֶׁן:

*Then he descended to Egypt — compelled by Divine decree. He sojourned there." This teaches that our father Jacob did not descend to Egypt to settle, but only to sojourn temporarily, as it says: "They (the sons of Jacob) said to Pharaoh, 'We have come to sojourn in this land because there is no pasture for the flocks of your servants, because the famine is severe in the land of Canaan. And now, please let your servants dwell in the land of Goshen.'"*

### BIMTEI ME'AT

The next paragraph states: *seventy people accompanied Ya'akov into Egypt but now they are many.*

Each of these seventy people represented one of the seventy nations of the world. These seventy people were responsible for giving their respective nations their spiritual Light and sustenance. The phrase *but now there are many* signifies the transference of responsibility. Each person on the planet would now be responsible for making his or her own connections to the Light.

With this personal responsibility comes global responsibility. When the destruction of the Temple occurred, it became necessary for each person to build and place his or her own "rock" back in the temple in order for it be reconstructed. We can achieve this through our personal correction and transformation of character. If one places a heavy rock on top of a weak rock, the weaker rock collapses and the Final Temple will never be built. What causes this heaviness? Ego. Everyone must let go of ego through spiritual work. All of us, whether we are a great and holy rabbi or a factory worker, are equal in the eyes of God. If we keep this consciousness of equality and no ego emblazoned in our hearts, our own rock will stand solid and firm with all the other rocks on top and below it. This will lead to the final appearance of the Temple.

בִּמְתֵי מְעָט, כְּמָה שֶׁנֶּאֱמַר מ״ה, בְּשִׁבְעִים נֶפֶשׁ יָרְדוּ אֲבֹתֶיךָ

מִצְרָיְמָה מּצר־ וְעַתָּה שָׂמְךָ יְהֹוָהֵאלֹהֶיךָ אֱלֹהֶיךָ ילה כְּכוֹכְבֵי

הַשָּׁמַיִם י״פ טל לָרֹב:

*They descended with few people, as it is written: "With seventy persons your forefathers descended to Egypt, and now Hashem, your God, has made you as numerous as the stars of heaven."*

### VYHEE SHAM
The Hagaddah says *and you were there [Egypt], a great nation.*

This means, even when we were in Egypt, surrounded by negativity, we didn't succumb to the evil. We can look Satan in the eye. We can look our addictions, fears, and phobias in the eye. And we know that we can overcome them.

וַיְהִי שָׁם לְגוֹי, מְלַמֵּד שֶׁהָיוּ יִשְׂרָאֵל מְצֻיָּנִים שָׁם: גָּדוֹל

עָצוּם, כְּמָה שֶׁנֶּאֱמַר מ״ה, וּבְנֵי יִשְׂרָאֵל פָּרוּ וַיִּשְׁרְצוּ וַיִּרְבּוּ

וַיַּעַצְמוּ בִּמְאֹד מְאֹד וַתִּמָּלֵא הָאָרֶץ אֹתָם:

*There he became a nation. This teaches that the Israelites were distinctive there. Great and mighty was the nation, as it says: "And the children of Israel were fruitful, increased greatly, multiplied, and became very, very mighty; and the land was filled with them."*

### VA'RAV
The Kabbalists learn from this paragraph that the importance of the Torah is not in the literal word itself but within the inner meaning of the word as revealed by the Talmud, the Midrash, and the Zohar.

The physical Torah is not real. It's a code. The Zohar deciphers this code. Without the spiritual understanding of the Torah, it means nothing. This connection helps us decipher the spiritual secrets of the Torah and the spiritual secrets of our own life. In other words, we will begin to see the spiritual laws at work in our life – the order beneath the chaos.

וָרֶב, כְּמָה מ״ה שֶׁנֶּאֱמַר, רְבָבָה כְּצֶמַח הַשָּׂדֶה נְתַתִּיךְ וַתִּרְבִּי

וַתִּגְדְּלִי וַתָּבֹאִי בַּעֲדִי עֲדָיִים שָׁדַיִם נָכֹנוּ וּשְׂעָרֵךְ צִמֵּחַ וְאַתְּ

עֵרֹם וְעֶרְיָה: וָאֶעֱבֹר עָלַיִךְ וָאֶרְאֵךְ מִתְבּוֹסֶסֶת בְּדָמָיִךְ

וָאֹמַר לָךְ בְּדָמַיִךְ חֲיִי וָאֹמַר לָךְ בְּדָמַיִךְ חֲיִי: וַיָּרֵעוּ אֹתָנוּ

הַמִּצְרִים מ״ר וַיְעַנּוּנוּ וַיִּתְּנוּ עָלֵינוּ עֲבֹדָה קָשָׁה:

*As it says, they were numerous: "I made you as numerous as the plants of the field; you grew and developed, and became charming, beautiful of figure, and your hair grew long, but you were naked and bare. And I passed over you and saw you rolling in your blood and I said to you: 'Through your blood shall you live.' And I said to you: 'Through your blood shall you live.' The Egyptians did evil to us, and afflicted us, and imposed hard labor upon us."*

### VAYAREU

The word *Vayareu* comes from the word *Reiya,* which means "friend." All too often, the negative side becomes our friend. The Satan makes negative actions likable and friendly to us.

There is another aspect to the word *friend:* Every time we begin a new relationship, we must pause for a moment and ask, "What do we really want from this relationship? Is it merely to fulfill our own ego and *desire-to-receive?*" It might be the in thing to hang out with certain people. Satan has a direct hand in this kind of friendship. Sooner or later, these new "friends" will bring you down. Fulfilling and lasting relationships must be based upon a mutual desire to reveal spiritual Light and positive energy into our world, not gratifying the ego. Real friends help each other grow spiritually. There is unconditional caring and an interdependence as both sides help one another to become better and more spiritually balanced people. When we associate with the wrong people, we always end up in trouble. This paragraph takes away the power of Satan so that he won't be able to influence us into befriending people for all the wrong reasons.

וַיָּרֵעוּ אֹתָנוּ הַמִּצְרִים מ״ר, כְּמָה מ״ה שֶׁנֶּאֱמַר, הָבָה נִתְחַכְּמָה

לוֹ פֶּן יִרְבֶּה יהה יהוה וְהָיָה כִּי תִקְרֶאנָה מִלְחָמָה וְנוֹסַף גַּם

הוּא עַל שֹׂנְאֵינוּ וְנִלְחַם בָּנוּ וְעָלָה מִן הָאָרֶץ:

*As it is stated, the Egyptians did evil to us: "Let us deal with them wisely lest they multiply and, if we happen to be at war, they may join our enemies and fight against us and then leave the country."*

### VAY'ANUNU

The beginning of this paragraph is in plural, and the end is in singular. The Kabbalists explain that the plural refers to the people in Egypt who were in bondage. The singular relates to the Light of God inside each person that was also held in bondage. By remaining in bondage, we literally imprison God, preventing His Light from being illuminated. Do we really want that liability hanging over our heads? This paragraph awakens this idea within us, motivating us to seek our own freedom for the purpose of sharing our Light with others.

וַיְעַנּוּנוּ, כְּמָה מ״ה שֶׁנֶּאֱמַר, וַיָּשִׂימוּ עָלָיו שָׂרֵי מִסִּים לְמַעַן עַנֹּתוֹ בְּסִבְלֹתָם וַיִּבֶן עָרֵי מִסְכְּנוֹת לְפַרְעֹה אֶת פִּתֹם וְאֶת רַעַמְסֵס:

*As it is stated, they afflicted us: "They let taskmasters over them in order to oppress them with their burdens; and they built Pithom and Ra'amses as treasure cities for Pharaoh."*

### VAY'ITNU

It says, *they gave us hard work.* We know from the Torah that every time the Israelites encountered hardships in the desert, they pleaded with Moses to take them back into Egypt, prompting the question, "How difficult could it have really been in Egypt?" The Zohar explains that slavery was not one of physicality but one of the soul and mind. The Egyptians bombarded us with black magic and negative thoughts and fed our ego. The Israelites lived this way without any regard to the spiritual consequences of their behavior. The concept of spiritual Light never entered the equation. Freedom means liberation from the negative thoughts and limited consciousness that confines us to such a narrow view of life and all that life can offer us. Freedom means breaking away from our ego-driven, self-centered thinking to embrace a positive, holistic view of the world and the cosmos.

וַיִּתְּנוּ עָלֵינוּ עֲבוֹדָה קָשָׁה, כְּמָה מ״ה שֶׁנֶּאֱמַר, וַיַּעֲבִדוּ מִצְרַיִם מצ־ אֶת בְּנֵי יִשְׂרָאֵל בְּפָרֶךְ: וַנִּצְעַק אֶל יְהֹוָהﭏﭏﭏ אֱלֹהֵי דמב אֲבֹתֵינוּ וַיִּשְׁמַע יְהֹוָהﭏﭏ אֶת קֹלֵנוּ וַיַּרְא אֶת עָנְיֵנוּ וְאֶת עֲמָלֵנוּ וְאֶת לַחֲצֵנוּ:

*As it is stated, they imposed hard labor upon us: "And the Egyptians subjugated the children of Israel with hard labor. We cried out to Hashem, our forefathers' God; and Hashem heard our cry and saw our deficiency, our trouble and our oppression."*

### VANITZAK

*We scream to God and He listened.* An intriguing remark that might lead a person to conclude that God listens only to those who scream. Does it mean that God does not care that we're hurting? Must we suffer to the point of screaming aloud before he finally answers us? Does God listen to some (the screamers), but not to others? The word *scream* refers to an inner scream of recognition and admittance that occurs within. God can help us only if we genuinely ask for help. The first prerequisite in asking for help is to recognize that our own negativity has lead us into chaos. Second, we must admit to ourselves that we alone cannot achieve any control or positive change without the Light of the Creator. This truth must scream out inside of us, breaking the silence of self-denial.

וַנִּצְעַק אֶל יְהֹוָהאדנייאהדונהי אֱלֹהֵי דמב אֲבוֹתֵינוּ, כְּמָה מ"ה שֶׁנֶּאֱמַר, וַיְהִי בַיָּמִים גלי הָרַבִּים הָהֵם וַיָּמָת מֶלֶךְ מִצְרַיִם מצר וַיֵּאָנְחוּ בְנֵי יִשְׂרָאֵל מִן הָעֲבֹדָה וַיִּזְעָקוּ וַתַּעַל שַׁוְעָתָם אֶל הָאֱלֹהִים ילה מִן הָעֲבֹדָה:

*We cried out to Hashem, our forefathers' God as it is stated: "During those many days, the king of Egypt died, and the children of Israel sighed because of the servitude and cried; and the cry because of the servitude rose up to God."*

### VAYISHMA

*And God listened.* Why do most of our prayers go unanswered? Unfortunately, most of us do not know the true methodology for igniting a prayer. Most prayers are switched on through the energy of Avraham, Isaac, and Ya'akov. The power of their names, the forces concealed inside the letters of their names, and our recognition that their spiritual energy remain in the cosmos today, are the ignition keys necessary to power our prayers. Through Avraham, Isaac, and Ya'akov, we are able to stand on the shoulders of giants and thrust our prayers into the Upper Worlds.

If, however, we believe that their names appear in our prayers simply for the sake of tradition and remembrance, we've lost the opportunity. This knowledge that we've just learned will, in itself, help ignite our prayers.[34]

וַיִּשְׁמַע יְהֹוָהאדנייאהדונהי אֶת קֹלֵנוּ, כְּמָה מ"ה שֶׁנֶּאֱמַר,

*And Hashem heard our cry as it is stated:*

---

34. The Baal Shem Tov was a great Kabbalist and rabbi who lived during the 18th century. There's a story that will help convey the principle at work in the connection of *Vayishma*. It is said that the Baal Shem Tov had a secret place in the forest where he would go every day to pray. This location was quite powerful, providing the Baal Shem Tov with a direct line to the Creator. This great sage also knew of a special prayer and meditation that had the power to reach the Creator, which, in turn, always generated a positive response. One of the Baal Shem Tov's students offered a prayer to the Creator and said, "I do not know the secret location where my holy master prays each day, but I do know the secret words and I know the forest in which he prayer. Therefore, please accept my own prayer." His prayers were accepted. Another student offered his prayer to God and said, "I do not know the secret words of my master, nor do I know the location of his prayers, but I do know a man who knows the forest in which my master prays." His prayers were answered. Another student prayed to God, saying, "I do not know the secrets words, the secret location or the forest where my master prays, but I do know a man who knows the forest where my master prays. Please accept my prayer on their merit." The young man's prayers were answered. By invoking the names of *Avraham, Isaac,* and *Ya'akov* in our prayer, we are asking God to accept it on the merit of these great patriarchs.

וַיִּשְׁמַע אֱלֹהִים יְלֹה אֶת נַאֲקָתָם וַיִּזְכֹּר אֱלֹהִים יְלֹה אֶת

בְּרִיתוֹ אֶת אַבְרָהָם רמ״חוחכמה אֶת יִצְחָק ד״פ ב״ן וְאֶת יַעֲקֹב:

*"God heard their sigh, and God recalled Its covenant with Abraham, with Isaac, and with Jacob."*

## VA'YA'AR

*God saw our pain.* This refers to a spiritual level that we all have to reach, which is to feel the pain of others. When God sees the pain of the people, it is as if God Himself is experiencing the same amount of pain, no different than a parent feels the pain of a child. If a friend or acquaintance of ours broke an arm, would we really feel the same pain in our arm?

That's the spiritual level we are striving for. Kabbalah teaches us that all the souls of humanity descend from the one unified soul of Adam. Accordingly, we are not striving to feel the pain of others because it is a nice, spiritual thing to do. The real reason is that every person is actually a part of ourselves on a deeper level of reality. When you have a cut on your arm, your entire body reacts and responds to try and heal it. The same principle is at work here.

וַיַּרְא אֶת עָנְיֵנוּ, זוֹ פְּרִישׁוּת דֶּרֶךְ ב״פ יב״ק אֶרֶץ מ״ה כָּמָה.

שֶׁנֶּאֱמַר, וַיַּרְא אֱלֹהִים יְלֹה אֶת בְּנֵי יִשְׂרָאֵל וַיֵּדַע אֱלֹהִים יְלֹה:

*Hashem saw our deficiency – that is, the disruption of family life As it is stated: "God saw the children of Israel and God knew."*

## VE'ET AMALEINU

*These are the children.* It's important to properly teach our children the spiritual lessons of life, because they will follow the path we set for them, whether we know it or not. Even while they sleep, our children are still affected by our spiritual actions. The Ari, in his Kabbalistic treatise *The Gates of Reincarnation,* explains that part of our soul comes from our mother, and part comes from our father. There is always an unseen spiritual link between both parents and the child. We must learn to teach our children, not in the do-as-I-say-but-not-as-I-do system of schooling, but rather in a spiritual manner where we set the example through our actions, both seen and unseen.

וְאֶת עֲמָלֵנוּ, אֵלּוּ הַבָּנִים. כָּמָה מ״ה שֶׁנֶּאֱמַר, וַיְצַו פַּרְעֹה

לְכָל יה אדני עַמּוֹ לֵאמֹר כָּל יל׳ הַבֵּן הַיִּלּוֹד הַיְאֹרָה

תַּשְׁלִיכֻהוּ וְכָל הַבַּת תְּחַיּוּן:

*And our trouble, which refers to the children. As it is stated: "Every son that is born, you shall cast into the river, but every daughter you shall let live."*

## V'ET LACHAT'ZENU

The sages explain that *V'et Lachat'zenu* refers to the term *our pressure.* This pressure refers to the forces of spiritual change. The pressure can be self-imposed – we choose to shut down our reactive impulses. Or the pressure can come from difficult external circumstances. Being held in bondage in Egypt is reactive pressure designed to provoke change through pain. We can avoid the reactive path through the power of this paragraph. Rav Ashlag teaches us that these two paths are always available to us. This paragraph gives us the strength and awareness to always recognize and choose the proactive path and avoid the path of torment and suffering.

וְאֶת לַחֲצֵנוּ, זוּ הַדְּחַק. כְּמָה מ״ה שֶׁנֶּאֱמַר, וְגַם רָאִיתִי אֶת

הַלַּחַץ אֲשֶׁר מִצְרַיִם מצר לוֹחֲצִים אֹתָם: וַיּוֹצִאֵנוּ יְהֹוָ(אדנيااهدونהי)

מִמִּצְרַיִם מצר בְּיָד חֲזָקָה וּבִזְרֹעַ נְטוּיָה וּבְמֹרָא גָּדֹל

וּבְאֹתוֹת וּבְמֹפְתִים:

*And our oppression, which refers to verbal pressure, as it is stated: "And I have seen how the Egyptians are oppressing them." "Hashem brought us out of Egypt with a mighty hand and with an outstretched arm, with great awe, with signs and wonders."*

## VAYOTZI'ENU

*God took us out from Egypt without any intermediaries, angels, or messengers.* It was God Himself who freed us in Egypt. This opportunity occurs once a year, on Passover, when God Himself comes down to free us from our slavery to our reactive nature. We must not squander this opportunity to connect to this great Light since our slavery is the root of all the chaos in our life.

We must also arouse a sense of appreciation that God is connecting to us directly. Normally, God works through intermediaries such as Avraham, Isaac, and Ya'akov or the various angels who inhabit the spiritual atmosphere. Awakening an appreciation for this direct connection helps to preserve it. It's human nature to appreciate something only after we have lost it. This section helps prevent that from happening.

וַיּוֹצִאֵנוּ יְהֹוָ(אדני̇יאاהדונהי) מִמִּצְרַיִם מצר, לֹא עַל יְדֵי מַלְאָךְ וְלֹא

עַל יְדֵי שָׂרָף וְלֹא עַל יְדֵי שָׁלִיחַ. אֶלָּא הַקָּדוֹשׁ בָּרוּךְ הוּא

בִּכְבוֹדוֹ וּבְעַצְמוֹ. שֶׁנֶּאֱמַר, וְעָבַרְתִּי בְאֶרֶץ מִצְרַיִם מצר

בַּלַּיְלָה מלה הַזֶּה והו וְהִכֵּיתִי כָל ילי בְּכוֹר בְּאֶרֶץ מִצְרַיִם מצר

מֵאָדָם וְעַד בְּהֵמָה לכב וּבְכָל לכב אֱלֹהֵי לכב מצב מִצְרַיִם מצר

אֶעֱשֶׂה שְׁפָטִים אֲנִי אני יְהֹוָ(אדनי̇יאاהדונהי):

*Hashem brought us out of Egypt — not through an angel, not through a seraph, and not through a messenger. But the Holy One, Blessed be He, in Its glory and by Itself, As it says: "I will pass through the land of Egypt on that night; I will slay all the firstborn in the land of Egypt from man to beast; and upon all the gods of Egypt I will execute judgment; I, Hashem."*

## V'AVARTI

*God went through Egypt during this night and killed all the first born.* Taken literally, this verse almost makes God appear evil. The spiritual meaning hidden inside this verse concerns the universal law of cause and effect. God does not punish, contrary to 2,000 years of belief.[35] We do it to ourselves. The Egyptians swore to massacre the first born of the Israelites. The cosmos works like a mirror. Curse in the mirror and the image curses back. Smile in the mirror and the reflection smiles back. We have been given the control and free will to interact with the cosmos in any way we choose. Kabbalah merely teaches us the most productive and fulfilling way to make our interactions – by setting aside our ego and showing care and compassion for others.

וְעָבַרְתִּי בְאֶרֶץ מִצְרַיִם מצֹ- בַּלַּיְלָה מלה הַזֶּה והוּ, אֲנִי אני וְלֹא

מַלְאָךְ. וְהִכֵּיתִי כָל ילֹ- בְּכוֹר בְּאֶרֶץ מִצְרַיִם מצֹ- אֲנִי אני וְלֹא

שָׂרָף. וּבְכָל לכב אֱלֹהֵי דמב מִצְרַיִם מצֹ- אֶעֱשֶׂה שְׁפָטִים אֲנִי אני

וְלֹא הַשָּׁלִיחַ. אֲנִי יְהֹוָה אדנֹי-אהדונהי אֲנִי אני הוּא אני וְלֹא אַחֵר:

*"I will pass throughthe land of Egypt on that night," not "I and an angel" "I will slay all the firstborn in the land of Egypt," not "I and a seraph"; "And upon all the gods of Egypt will I execute judgments," not "I and the messenger." "I, Hashem," not any other.*

## B'YAD CHAZAKAH

Kabbalistically, there are three Hands, or three energy forces, at work in the cosmos. One is called the Big Hand (*Yad Hagdolah*), which is Right Column.[36] We connect to the Big Hand through the splitting of the Red Sea. The second hand is called Strong Hand (*Yad Hachazakah*), which is Left Column. This is the column we are connecting to right now through the *Hagaddah*. The Strong Hand connects to immortality.[37] The third Hand is

---

35. A person plugs a computer into his wall socket and makes a fortune selling goods on the Internet. The electricity in the socket is considered to be a positive and productive force that benefited this person's life. Another person sticks his finger into the same socket and electrocutes himself. Can we say that the intent of the electrical current was to punish the individual? Of course not. Did the nature of the electricity change in either scenario? No. What changed was the way the person connected to the energy. The Light of God works in the same manner. It is an ever present force of spiritual energy. If we behave proactively, with love and concern for others, this force generates Light in our lives. If we abuse others and behave reactively, we receive a jolt and shock. The problem is that we have been living life with our finger lodged in the light socket for 2,000 years. This is the law of cause and effect, and its purpose is to allow us the free will to change.

36. There are three forces built into the universe—the force of sharing (Right Column), the force of receiving (Left Column), and the force of balance (Central Column). These three forces exist both in the physical and spiritual worlds. Physically, they represent the proton (Right Column), the electron (Left Column), and the neutron (Central Column). These three subatomic particles are the building blocks of the atom. You need all three columns to create a circuit of energy both physically and spiritually.

37. 16th-century Kabbalist Rabbi Avraham Azulai wrote that the secrets of immortality will begin to emerge around the Hebrew calendar year of 5760—the year 2000. Immortality was always considered the great taboo in the medical sciences. Then suddenly, in 1998, the biotechnology firm Geron announced that it was able to produce immortal human stem cells in the laboratory. Stem cells

called Uplifted Hand *(Yad Ramah)*, which is Central Column. The Exodus from Egypt occurred through the Central Column of the Uplifted Hand.

בְּיָד וְחֲזָקָה, זוֹ הַדֶּבֶר. כְּמָה מ"ה שֶׁנֶּאֱמַר, הִנֵּה יַד יְהֹוָׇאדנּיֵאהדוִּנֹהי הוֹיָה בְּמִקְנְךָ אֲשֶׁר בַּשָּׂדֶה בַּסּוּסִים בַּחֲמֹרִים בַּגְּמַלִּים בַּבָּקָר וּבַצֹּאן דֶּבֶר כָּבֵד מְאֹד:

*With a mighty hand, which refers to the pestilence, as it is stated: "Behold, the hand of Hashem shall strike your cattle which are in the field, the horses, the donkeys, the camels, and the sheep" – a very severe pestilence.*

### UVI'ZROA

*The Satan's sword is outstretched over Jerusalem to destroy it.* Why is such a negative statement made in the Hagaddah? To teach us that on the original Passover, we did not completely finish our spiritual work. If we think we have, the Satan only gets stronger. Today, more than ever, we must come to grips with the realization that Judaism is not a religion, that the force of Satan is real, that our ego and reactive behavior is the root of all chaos. With this awareness, we can utilize Passover the way it was meant to be used – as a powerful weapon of freedom that can help us break free from the chains of our ego. That is the work still to be completed.

וּבִזְרֹעַ נְטוּיָה, זוֹ הַחֶרֶב. כְּמָה מ"ה שֶׁנֶּאֱמַר, וְחַרְבּוֹ ר"ת שְׁלוּפָה בְּיָדוֹ נְטוּיָה עַל יְרוּשָׁלָיִם.

*And with an outstretched arm, which refers to the sword, as it is stated: "His drawn sword in his hand, outstretched over Jerusalem."*

### UV'MORA

*With great fear.* The Hagaddah explains that this verse refers to the manifestation of the Shechinah, the presence of God in our physical realm. While in Egypt, we did not have a strong enough connection to the Shechinah because we were neck deep in our own negativity. We actually reached the 49th gate of evil.[38] Therefore, we did not really merit the Exodus from Egypt. During the 49 days *after* Passover, however, the Israelites cleansed each gate of negativity by working on themselves spiritually, signified by their tormenting journey through the desert.

When the Hagaddah says we connected to the Shechinah, it is not referring to ancient

---

are unique in that they are in an undifferentiated state allowing them to develop into a variety of other cells such as kidney or heart cells. Remarkably, these stem cells were found to be immortal.

Tom Okarma, Geron's VP of research and development, said, "The discovery that we are talking about is the derivation of human embryonic stem cells that are capable of developing into all cells and tissues of the body and are immortal. The cells are immortal. They will live forever."

38. There are fifty gates or fifty levels of negativity. Once a person reaches the fiftieth gate, he is evil personified. There is no turning back. His opportunity for change and transformation in his present lifetime has vanquished.

times in Egypt. It refers to the holiday of Shavuot, which occurs exactly 49 days after Passover.

וּבְמוֹרָא גָּדוֹל, זוֹ גִּלּוּי שְׁכִינָה. כְּמָה. כְּמָה מ״ה שֶׁנֶּאֱמַר, אוֹ הֲנִסָּה

אֱלֹהִים יה, לָבוֹא לָקַחַת לוֹ גוֹי מִקֶּרֶב גוֹי בְּמַסֹּת בְּאֹתֹת

וּבְמוֹפְתִים וּבְמִלְחָמָה וּבְיָד וַחֲזָקָה וּבִזְרוֹעַ נְטוּיָה וּבְמוֹרָאִים

גְּדֹלִים כְּכֹל אֲשֶׁר עָשָׂה לָכֶם יְהֹוָהאדניאהדונהי אֱלֹהֵיכֶם יה

בְּמִצְרַיִם מ״צ לְעֵינֶיךָ:

*And with great awe: This is the revelation of the Shechinah. As it is stated, "Has God ever attempted to take unto Itself a nation from the midst of other nation by trials, miraculous signs and wonders, by war, with a mighty hand, with outstretched arm, and with awesome revelations, as all that your God did for you in Egypt, before your eyes?"*

## UV'OTOT

*This is the rod.* From the time of Creation, Moshes' rod was built and charged with the power to achieve all the miracles that would come to pass during the time of slavery in Egypt. There's a story concerning the rod and Moshes' father-in-law, Yitro. The rod was lodged in the ground inside Yitro's home. Yitro offered a lot of money, along with the hand of his daughter in marriage, to anyone who could dislodge the rod from the ground. Yitro knew the staff possessed tremendous spiritual powers, beyond mortal comprehension. Engraved on the rod were the 72 Names of God[39] and the 42-Letter Name of God, the Ana B'koach.[40] When Moses came to the house of Yitro, he pulled the staff out of the ground. It was now released to its rightful owner. This connection gives us the power of miracles that the rod represents.

וּבְאֹתֹת, זֶה הַמַּטֶּה. כְּמָה מ״ה שֶׁנֶּאֱמַר, וְאֶת הַמַּטֶּה הַזֶּה והו

תִּקַּח בְּיָדְךָ אֲשֶׁר תַּעֲשֶׂה בּוֹ אֶת הָאֹתֹת:

*And with signs, which refers to the miracles performed with the staff: As it is stated, "Take this staff in your hand, that you may perform the miraculous signs with it."*

---

39. The 72 Names of God is a formula Moses used to engineer the miracles in Egypt. This formula was concealed inside the holy Zohar for more than 2,000 years. It consists of 72 three-letter sequences encoded inside the story of Exodus in the Torah. Each three-letter sequence gives us a particular power to overcome the numerous negative traits of human nature, in the same way that Moses used this spiritual technology to overpower the laws of mother nature.

40. Ana B'koach is another formula, built of 42 letters, that gives us the ability to transcend this physical world with all its limitations. Ana B'koach can literally remove the friction, barriers, and obstacles associated with our physical existence. It can inject order into chaos, remove the Satan's influence from our nature, generate financial sustenance, arouse unity and love for others, provide healing energy to the body and soul. We can recite or scan the Ana B'koach every day.

## UV'MOFTIM

This paragraph concerns the plague of the blood. Of all the Ten Plagues, it was the plague of the blood that demonstrated the distinction between Egypt and the Israelites and the ultimate power of God. For example, when drinking water, an Israelite would drink clear liquid while the water in the glass of the Egyptians transformed into blood. This paragraph gives us the power of protection during any onslaught of chaos, provided we remain spiritually connected.

וּבְמוֹפְתִים זֶה הַדָּם. כְּמָה ה"מ שֶׁנֶּאֱמַר. וְנָתַתִּי מוֹפְתִים

בַּשָּׁמַיִם י"ס טל וּבָאָרֶץ

*And with wonders, which alludes to the blood. As it is stated: "I will show wonders in the heavens and on the earth."*

While we recite the next four words, we pour wine from our cup

דָּם וָאֵשׁ וְתִימְרוֹת עָשָׁן:

*Blood and fire and columns of smoke*

דָּבָר ראה אַחֵר, בְּיָד חֲזָקָה שְׁתַּיִם. וּבִזְרֹעַ נְטוּיָה שְׁתַּיִם.

וּבְמֹרָא גָּדוֹל שְׁתַּיִם. וּבְאֹתוֹת שְׁתַּיִם. וּבְמוֹפְתִים שְׁתַּיִם.

*Another thing [another explanation of the preceding verse is that each phrase represents two plagues.] The mighty hand represents two plagues, the outstretched arm another two, the great awe another two, the signs another two, and the wonders another two.*

## THE TEN PLAGUES

The term *Ten Plagues* is a code signifying ten levels of energy that sustain the Klipot. Klipot are shells of negativity created by our negative deeds and actions. We call them shells because they trap sparks of Light, similar to the way a shell conceals a nut. Klipot actually steal sparks of Light from us every time we commit a misdeed. Klipot exist in each of the ten Sfirot, the ten dimensions that make up our reality. Each of the ten plagues that we now recite removes the Light from the Klipot in all ten dimensions. With their life-force cut off, the Klipot will die off, freeing us from their clutches.

According to Kabbalah, the Egyptians represent the Klipot. Why do the sages consider the Egyptians to be on such a low level? Even with all their black magic, their constant reactive behavior, and negative actions, do these traits warrant classifying them as the Klipot? No. The reason they represent the Klipot is because not one Egyptian treated even one Israelite or even another Egyptian with human dignity and sensitivity.

Rav Berg teaches us that if we do not treat people with human dignity, there will never be genuine freedom, fulfillment on earth, or peace among nations. Never. No matter how much we meditate, pray, and perform the rites and rituals, if we treat our friends and our enemies without any semblance of human compassion and sensitivity, it will lead us right back into chaos, mayhem, and destruction.

There are two holy names that help us with this process: *Yud Vav Hei final Caf* יוהך and *Caf Hei Taf* כהת.

אֵלוּ עֶשֶׂר מַכּוֹת שֶׁהֵבִיא הַקָּדוֹשׁ בָּרוּךְ הוּא

עַל הַמִּצְרִים מ״צ בְּמִצְרַיִם מ״צ וְאֵלוּ הֵן:

*These are the ten plagues that the Holy One, Blessed be He, brought upon the Egyptians in Egypt:*

As we recite each verse, we pour from the cup of wine

דָּם. צְפַרְדֵּעַ. כִּנִּים. עָרוֹב. דֶּבֶר. שְׁחִין. בָּרָד.

אַרְבֶּה. וְחֹשֶׁךְ. מַכַּת בְּכוֹרוֹת:

*Blood, frogs, vermin, wild beasts, pestilence, Boils, hail, locusts, darkness, and the deaths of the firstborn.*

### RABBI YEHUDA

After the Ten Plagues are recited, the great sage **Rabbi Yehuda** gave us an acronym. When we recite or pray from the Hagaddah, angels take our prayer to the Upper Worlds. They act as our transportation system. There are certain times when we don't want an intermediary. We need to go straight to the source. The Aramaic language is a code that the angels cannot understand.[41] Acronyms are another sequence of Hebrew letters that are above the comprehension of angels. Because the negative side of Satan also has angels that can influence and sabotage our connections, we employ Aramaic and acronyms when we want to bypass their "transportation routes." Codes, acronyms, and the Aramaic language are our super weapons in the battle against evil and the negative forces.

There is an interesting debate concerning how many plagues actually struck Egypt. **Rabbi Yossi** says there were ten plagues, and at the parting of the Red Sea there were another 50 plagues. **Rabbi Elieazer** says there were 40 in Egypt and 200 at the Red Sea. **Rabbi Akiva** says 50 in Egypt and 250 at the Sea.

Which one of these great sages is right? They are all right, on a deeper level of reality. The Kabbalists explain that when you add all the letters of the ten plagues together, you get 3,280. Numerically, this equals the amount of negative angels residing in our universe.

Each one of the Rabbis connected to a different path to destroy the negativity. Each used the holy name that connected to their soul. Each one of our souls connects to one or all of these paths. Thankfully, our path to destroy the Satan has already been paved by these great giants.

רַבִּי יְהוּדָה הָיָה ״הה נוֹתֵן בָּהֶם סִמָּנִים:

*Rabbi Yehuda abbreviated them by their Hebrew initials:*

---

41. Kol Nidre, which is recited on Yom Kippur, *the Zohar*, the Kaddish, and the Talmud are all written in Aramaic. Mmarriage certificates are also composed in Aramaic. This protects these holy connections and documents from any negative influences.

We pour a bit of wine three times from the cup

# דְּצַ"ךְ עֲדַ"שׁ בְּאַחַ"ב:

*D'tzach, Adash, B'achab*

We refill the cups. The wine that was removed is not used.

## RABBI YOSSI

Rabbi Yossi's name adds up to 386. The value of the holy name *Shin Pei Vav* שׁפוּ is also 386. We meditate upon this sequence before we recite **Rabbi Yossi's** words. The Kabbalists teach us that **Rabbi Yossi** is a spark of King David. The phrase *David, son of Yeshai* דוד בן ישׁי also equals 386.

רַבִּי יוֹסֵי הַגְּלִילִי אוֹמֵר: מִנַּיִן אַתָּה אוֹמֵר שֶׁלָּקוּ הַמִּצְרִים מצר

בְּמִצְרַיִם מצר עֶשֶׂר מַכּוֹת וְעַל הַיָּם ילי לָקוּ וַחֲמִשִּׁים מַכּוֹת.

בְּמִצְרַיִם מצר מַה מ"ה הוּא אוֹמֵר, וַיֹּאמְרוּ הַחַרְטֻמִּים אֶל

פַּרְעֹה אֶצְבַּע אֱלֹהִים ילה הִיא. וְעַל הַיָּם ילי מָה מ"ה הוּא

אוֹמֵר, וַיַּרְא יִשְׂרָאֵל אֶת הַיָּד וְזֶהוּ הַגְּדֹלָה אֲשֶׁר עָשָׂה

יְהֹוָאהדונהי בְּמִצְרַיִם מצר וַיִּירְאוּ הָעָם אֶת יְהֹוָאהדונהי

וַיַּאֲמִינוּ בַּיהֹוָאהדונהי וּבְמֹשֶׁה מהע עַבְדּוֹ: כַּמָּה מ"ה לָקוּ

בְּאֶצְבַּע עֶשֶׂר מַכּוֹת. אֱמוֹר מֵעַתָּה, בְּמִצְרַיִם מצר לָקוּ

עֶשֶׂר מַכּוֹת וְעַל הַיָּם ילי לָקוּ וַחֲמִשִּׁים מַכּוֹת:

*Rabbi Yosi the Galilean said, "How does one derive that the Egyptians were struck with ten plagues in Egypt, but with 50 plagues at the sea? Concerning the plagues in Egypt the Torah states: 'the magicians said to Pharaoh, "It is the finger of God."' However, of those at the sea, the Torah says: 'and Israel saw the great hand which Hashem laid upon the Egyptians, the people feared Hashem and believed in Hashem and in Moses, his servant.' How many plagues did they receive with the finger? Ten. From now on say, in Egypt they received ten plagues and on the sea they received fifty plagues."*

## RABBI ELIEZER

Rabbi Eliezer's name equals 530, the same numerical value as the holy name *Taf, Kof, Lamed* nmygr,. We mediate upon this name before we recite **Rabbi Eliezer's** discourse.

רַבִּי אֱלִיעֶזֶר אוֹמֵר: מִנַּיִן שֶׁכָּל מַכָּה וּמַכָּה שֶׁהֵבִיא

הַקָּדוֹשׁ בָּרוּךְ הוּא עַל הַמִּצְרִים מֵ"צ- בְּמִצְרַיִם מֵ"צ- הָיְתָה

שֶׁל אַרְבַּע מַכּוֹת. שֶׁנֶּאֱמַר, יְשַׁלַּח בָּם מ"ב- חֲרוֹן אַפּוֹ עֶבְרָה

וָזַעַם וְצָרָה מִשְׁלַחַת מַלְאֲכֵי רָעִים: עֶבְרָה אַחַת. וָזַעַם

שְׁתַּיִם. וְצָרָה שָׁלֹשׁ. מִשְׁלַחַת מַלְאֲכֵי רָעִים אַרְבַּע. אֱמוֹר

מֵעַתָּה, בְּמִצְרַיִם מֵ"צ- לָקוּ אַרְבָּעִים מַכּוֹת וְעַל הַיָּם יֵ"ל לָקוּ

מָאתַיִם מַכּוֹת:

*Rabbi Eliezer says: "How does one derive that every plague that the Holy One, Blessed be He, inflicted upon the Egyptians in Egypt was equal to four plagues? For it is written: 'It sent upon them Its fierce anger: wrath, fury, and trouble and a band of emissaries of evil.' [Since each plague in Egypt consists of] (1) wrath, (2) fury, (3) trouble, and (4) a band of emissaries of evil, in Egypt they were struck by 40 plagues, and on the sea they were struck by 200 plagues."*

### RABBI AKIVA

Rabbi Akiva's value equals 395, which is identical to the holy name עצה.

רַבִּי עֲקִיבָא אוֹמֵר: מִנַּיִן שֶׁכָּל מַכָּה וּמַכָּה שֶׁהֵבִיא

הַקָּדוֹשׁ בָּרוּךְ הוּא עַל הַמִּצְרִים מֵ"צ- בְּמִצְרַיִם מֵ"צ- הָיְתָה

שֶׁל וָחֲמֵשׁ מַכּוֹת. שֶׁנֶּאֱמַר, יְשַׁלַּח בָּם מ"ב- חֲרוֹן אַפּוֹ עֶבְרָה

וָזַעַם וְצָרָה מִשְׁלַחַת מַלְאֲכֵי רָעִים: חֲרוֹן אַפּוֹ אַחַת.

עֶבְרָה שְׁתַּיִם. וָזַעַם שָׁלֹשׁ. וְצָרָה אַרְבַּע. מִשְׁלַחַת מַלְאֲכֵי

רָעִים וָחֲמֵשׁ. אֱמוֹר מֵעַתָּה בְּמִצְרַיִם מֵ"צ- לָקוּ וָחֲמִשִּׁים

מַכּוֹת וְעַל הַיָּם יֵ"ל לָקוּ וָחֲמִשִּׁים וּמָאתַיִם מַכּוֹת:

*Rabbi Akiva said: "How does one derive that every plague that the Holy One, Blessed be He, inflicted upon the Egyptians in Egypt was equal to five plagues? For it is written: 'It sent upon them Its fierce anger, wrath, fury, and trouble and a band of emissaries of evil.' (Since each plague in Egypt consists of) (1) fierce anger, (2) wrath, (3) fury, (4) trouble, and (5) a band of emissaries of evil, in Egypt they were struck by fifty plagues, and on the sea they were struck by 250 plagues."*

## DAIYENU

*It is enough.* The concept of appreciation is at work in this song. We must be content with all that we have at the present moment – *It is enough* – for God gives us what we truly need and not necessarily what we want. Our consciousness during this song should be one of appreciation for all we have in order to ensure that we never lose it.

כַּמָּה מ"ה מַעֲלוֹת טוֹבוֹת לַמָּקוֹם עָלֵינוּ:

אִלּוּ הוֹצִיאָנוּ מִמִּצְרַיִם מצר, וְלֹא עָשָׂה בָהֶם שְׁפָטִים דַּיֵּנוּ:

אִלּוּ עָשָׂה בָהֶם שְׁפָטִים, וְלֹא עָשָׂה בֵאלֹהֵיהֶם דַּיֵּנוּ:

אִלּוּ עָשָׂה בֵאלֹהֵיהֶם, וְלֹא הָרַג אֶת בְּכוֹרֵיהֶם דַּיֵּנוּ:

אִלּוּ הָרַג אֶת בְּכוֹרֵיהֶם, וְלֹא נָתַן לָנוּ מום אֶת מָמוֹנָם דַּיֵּנוּ:

אִלּוּ נָתַן לָנוּ מום אֶת מָמוֹנָם, וְלֹא קָרַע לָנוּ מום אֶת הַיָּם ילי דַּיֵּנוּ:

אִלּוּ קָרַע לָנוּ מום אֶת הַיָּם ילי, וְלֹא הֶעֱבִירָנוּ בְתוֹכוֹ בֶּחָרָבָה דַּיֵּנוּ:

אִלּוּ הֶעֱבִירָנוּ בְתוֹכוֹ בֶּחָרָבָה, וְלֹא שִׁקַּע צָרֵינוּ בְּתוֹכוֹ דַּיֵּנוּ:

אִלּוּ שִׁקַּע צָרֵינוּ בְּתוֹכוֹ, וְלֹא סִפֵּק צָרְכֵּנוּ בַּמִּדְבָּר אַרְבָּעִים שָׁנָה דַּיֵּנוּ:

*The Omnipresent has bestowed so many favors upon us! Had He brought us out of Egypt, but not executed judgments against the Egyptians, it would have sufficed us. Had He executed judgments against the Egyptians, but not upon their gods, it would have sufficed us. Had He executed judgments against their gods, but not slain their firstborn, it would have sufficed us. Had He slain their firstborn, but not given us their wealth, it would have sufficed us. Had He given us their wealth, but not split the sea for us, it would have sufficed us. Had He split the sea for us, but not led us through it on dry land, it would have sufficed us. Had He led us through it on dry land, but not drowned our oppressors in it, it would have sufficed us. Had He drowned our oppressors in it, but not provided for our needs in the desert for forty years, it would have sufficed us.*

אִלוּ סִפֵּק צָרְכֵנוּ בַּמִּדְבָּר אַרְבָּעִים שָׁנָה,

וְלֹא הֶאֱכִילָנוּ אֶת הַמָּן     דַּיֵּנוּ:

אִלוּ הֶאֱכִילָנוּ אֶת הַמָּן, וְלֹא נָתַן לָנוּ מ= אֶת הַשַּׁבָּת   דַּיֵּנוּ:

אִלוּ נָתַן לָנוּ מ= אֶת הַשַּׁבָּת, וְלֹא קֵרְבָנוּ לִפְנֵי

הַר סִינַי נמם      דַּיֵּנוּ:

אִלוּ קֵרְבָנוּ לִפְנֵי הַר סִינַי ה נמם, וְלֹא נָתַן לָנוּ מ=

אֶת הַתּוֹרָה      דַּיֵּנוּ:

אִלוּ נָתַן לָנוּ מ= אֶת הַתּוֹרָה, וְלֹא הִכְנִיסָנוּ

לְאֶרֶץ יִשְׂרָאֵל      דַּיֵּנוּ:

אִלוּ הִכְנִיסָנוּ לְאֶרֶץ יִשְׂרָאֵל, וְלֹא בָנָה לָנוּ מ=

אֶת בֵּית ב"פ ראה הַבְּחִירָה      דַּיֵּנוּ:

*Had He provided for our needs in the desert for forty years, but not fed us the Manna, it would have sufficed us. Had He fed us the Manna, but not given us the Shabbat, it would have sufficed us. Had He given us the Shabbat, but not brought us before Mount Sinai, it would have sufficed us. Had He brought us before Mount Sinai, but not given us the Torah, it would have sufficed us. Had He given us the Torah, but not brought us into the land of Israel, it would have sufficed us. Had He brought us into the land of Israel, but not built the temple for us, it would have sufficed us.*

### AL ACHAT

**God has given everything to us.** We must now make a sincere effort to appreciate all that is still coming to us. This is a direct reference to the coming of the Final Temple. When the temple finally appears, all chaos, death, and decay will come to an end.

Rav Berg teaches us that there is one secret for hastening this new reality: Believe it, and you will see it. Remember, Satan's favorite catch phrase is "I'll believe it when I see it."

עַל אַחַת כַּמָּה מ"ה וְכַמָּה מ"ה טוֹבָה אכא כְּפוּלָה וּמְכֻפֶּלֶת

לַמָּקוֹם עָלֵינוּ.

*Thus, how much more should we be grateful to the Omnipresent for all the numerous favors He showered upon us:*

שֶׁהוֹצִיאָנוּ מִמִּצְרַיִם מצר. וְעָשָׂה בָהֶם שְׁפָטִים. וְעָשָׂה

בֵאלֹהֵיהֶם. וְהָרַג אֶת בְּכוֹרֵיהֶם. וְנָתַן לָנוּ מום אֶת מָמוֹנָם.

וְקָרַע לָנוּ מום אֶת הַיָּם ילי. וְהֶעֱבִירָנוּ בְּתוֹכוֹ בֶּחָרָבָה.

וְשִׁקַּע צָרֵינוּ בְּתוֹכוֹ. וְסִפֵּק צָרְכֵנוּ בַּמִּדְבָּר אַרְבָּעִים שָׁנָה.

וְהֶאֱכִילָנוּ אֶת הַמָּן. וְנָתַן לָנוּ מום אֶת הַשַּׁבָּת. וְקֵרְבָנוּ לִפְנֵי

הַר סִינַי נמס. וְנָתַן לָנוּ מום אֶת הַתּוֹרָה. וְהִכְנִיסָנוּ לְאֶרֶץ

יִשְׂרָאֵל. וּבָנָה לָנוּ מום אֶת בֵּית ב"פ ראה הַבְּוֹחִירָה לְכַפֵּר עַל

כָּל ילי עֲוֹנוֹתֵינוּ:

*brought us out of Egypt, executed judgments against the Egyptians and against their gods, slew their firstborn, gave us their wealth, split the sea for us, let us through it on dry land, drowned our oppressors in it, provided for our needs in the desert for 40 years, fed us the Manna, gave us the Shabbat, brought us before Mount Sinai, gave us the Torah, brought us to the land of Israel, and built us the temple – to atone for our sins.*

### RABAN GAMLIEL
The Hagaddah tells us that if we do not recite the following three words: *Pesach, Matzah,* and *Maror,* we have not fulfilled our obligation to God. In Kabbalah, there is no such thing as an obligation to appease God. Everything is for our own benefit. The obligation is to our own soul and our own desire to achieve fulfillment.

רַבָּן גַּמְלִיאֵל הָיָה יהה אוֹמֵר: כָּל ילי שֶׁלֹּא אָמַר שְׁלֹשָׁה

דְּבָרִים אֵלּוּ בַּפֶּסַח לֹא יָצָא יְדֵי חוֹבָתוֹ, וְאֵלּוּ הֵן:

## פֶּסַח. מַצָּה. וּמָרוֹר:

*Raban Gamliel used to say: "Whoever has not mentioned the following three things on Passover, has not done his job, namely: Pesach – the Passover offering, Matzah – the unleavened bread, and Maror – the bitter herbs.*

### PESACH
The original Pesach included the practice of taking a sacrifice to the Temple. The physical temple is no longer standing, so we must become the sacrifice of our reactive behavior.[42]

---

42. We must look within and sacrifice at least one of our negative traits. If it's easy and comfortable, it is not considered a sacrifice. This sacrifice could involve going to a friend or family member during

פֶּסַח שֶׁהָיוּ אֲבוֹתֵינוּ אוֹכְלִים בִּזְמַן שֶׁבֵּית הַמִּקְדָּשׁ רא בּ״פ

הָיָה יהה קַיָּם עַל שׁוּם מָה. מ״ה. עַל שׁוּם שֶׁפָּסַח הַקָּדוֹשׁ

בָּרוּךְ הוּא עַל בָּתֵּי אֲבוֹתֵינוּ בְּמִצְרַיִם. מצר. שֶׁנֶּאֱמַר,

וַאֲמַרְתֶּם זֶבַח פֶּסַח הוּא לַיהוה אהדונהיאהדונהי אֲשֶׁר פָּסַח עַל בָּתֵּי

בְנֵי יִשְׂרָאֵל בְּמִצְרַיִם מצר. בְּנָגְפּוֹ אֶת מִצְרַיִם וְאֶת בָּתֵּינוּ מצר.

הִצִּיל וַיִּקֹּד הָעָם וַיִּשְׁתַּחֲוּוּ׃

*Passover that our fathers eat the offering during the time of the temple? Because the Holy One, Blessed be He, passed over the houses of our fathers in Egypt, as it is says: "You shall say, 'It is a Passover offering for Hashem, which passed over the houses of the children of Israel in Egypt when He struck the Egyptians and spared our houses' – and the people bowed down and prostrated themselves."*

## MATZAH

According to tradition, there was no time for the Israelites to allow their bread to rise, so they were left with Matzah. This situation is merely the effect and not the spiritual cause. Kabbalah asks why events unfolded this way in the first place. The Ari teaches us that we must never examine the effect but instead probe to the seed level, the hidden cause: Matzah is bread without ego. Bread expands and rises (like our egos) because it contains enormous spiritual energy. With Matzah, there is an aspect of restriction at work. Matzah is an instrument that gives us the strength to restrict our ego for the entire year.

### We show the Matzah to everyone

מַצָּה זוֹ שֶׁאָנוּ אוֹכְלִים עַל שׁוּם מָה. מ״ה. עַל שׁוּם שֶׁלֹּא

הִסְפִּיק בְּצֵקָם שֶׁל אֲבוֹתֵינוּ לְהַחֲמִיץ עַד שֶׁנִּגְלָה עֲלֵיהֶם

מֶלֶךְ מַלְכֵי הַמְּלָכִים הַקָּדוֹשׁ בָּרוּךְ הוּא וּגְאָלָם. שֶׁנֶּאֱמַר,

וַיֹּאפוּ אֶת הַבָּצֵק אֲשֶׁר הוֹצִיאוּ מִמִּצְרַיִם מצר. עֻגֹת מַצּוֹת

*Matzah. Why do we eat this unleavened bread? Because the dough of our fathers did not have time to become leavened before the King of Kings, the Holy One, Blessed be He, revealed Itself to them and redeemed them, as it is written: "They baked the dough which they had brought out of Egypt into unleavened bread,*

---

Passover and working out a difficult situation by giving up your ego and admitting we are wrong. We might approach a friend or enemy and confess our jealousies. The harder it is, the more Light we will receive. According to the principles of Kabbalah, we will be amazed at the sudden turn of events and responses we will receive from the people we approach. The moment we lower our guard, remove our ego, and offer someone genuine Light through our own sacrifice and humility, they will shock us and respond positively.

כִּי לֹא חָמֵץ כִּי גֹרְשׁוּ מִמִּצְרַיִם ־מ־ וְלֹא יָכְלוּ לְהִתְמַהְמֵהַּ
וְגַם צֵדָה לֹא עָשׂוּ לָהֶם:

*for it had not fermented, because they were driven out of Egypt and could not delay, nor had they prepared any provisions for the way."*

## MAROR

Maror is the same numerical value as the word *death*. For us to reach a state of immortality, which we can achieve on Shavout, we must taste death. The Maror is our instrument for tasting death. Sadly, some people's lives are worse than death. By slowly chewing the Maror and embracing the intense pain it generates, we can proactively taste death and therefore gradually remove the force of death from our lives. Each chew of the Maror, by every person on the planet keeping Passover, brings us another step closer to genuine immortality.

We show the maror to everyone

מָרוֹר זֶה שֶׁאָנוּ אוֹכְלִים עַל שׁוּם מָה ־מ־ה. עַל שׁוּם שֶׁמֵּרְרוּ
הַמִּצְרִים ־מ־ אֶת וַיֵּי אֲבוֹתֵינוּ בְּמִצְרַיִם ־מ־. שֶׁנֶּאֱמַר, וַיְמָרְרוּ
אֶת וַיֵּיהֶם בַּעֲבֹדָה קָשָׁה בְּחֹמֶר וּבִלְבֵנִים וּבְכָל ־לב־ עֲבֹדָה
בַּשָּׂדֶה אֶת כָּל ־י־ עֲבֹדָתָם אֲשֶׁר עָבְדוּ בָהֶם בְּפָרֶךְ:

*Maror. Why do we eat this bitter herb? Because the Egyptians embittered the lives of our fathers in Egypt, as it says: "They embittered their lives with hard labor, with mortar and bricks, and with all manner of labor in the field; whatever service which they performed with hard labor."*

## B'CHOL

*He went out of Egypt.* The ultimate secret to the power of the Seder night is revealed here. The magic key to obtaining freedom from slavery in Egypt is to know and accept that you *are* in Egypt.[43] Contrary to 2,000 years of tradition, the Seder night is not about the retelling of a story that occurred 3,300 years ago. The energy of freedom and the reality of slavery is occurring at this very moment. The purpose of the Seder night is to free us from the various bondage of our present life.

---

43. Egypt is a code word for our reactive behavior. Our ego. Low-self esteem. Lack of confidence. Over-confidence. Need for acceptance. Fear. Phobias. Jealousy. Obsession. Uncontrolled ambition. All these qualities are merely various names for the prisons that enslave us. Any aspect of our nature that controls us is "Egypt." Our problem is denial. We fail to recognize that we are slaves to these desires. Being aware that we are in "Egypt," that we are under the control of these reactive drives, is the key that unlocks the cell door.

בְּכָל לכב דּוֹר וָדוֹר ריי וַיָּב אָדָם לִרְאוֹת אֶת עַצְמוֹ כְּאִלּוּ
הוּא יָצָא מִמִּצְרָיִם מצר, שֶׁנֶּאֱמַר, וְהִגַּדְתָּ לְבִנְךָ בַּיּוֹם נגד, ז
הַהוּא לֵאמֹר בַּעֲבוּר זֶה עָשָׂה יְהוָֹהאדישאדוני לִי בְּצֵאתִי
מִמִּצְרָיִם מצר: שֶׁלֹּא אֶת אֲבוֹתֵינוּ בִּלְבָד גָּאַל הַקָּדוֹשׁ
בָּרוּךְ הוּא, אֶלָּא אַף אוֹתָנוּ גָּאַל עִמָּהֶם. שֶׁנֶּאֱמַר, וְאוֹתָנוּ
הוֹצִיא מִשָּׁם לְמַעַן הָבִיא אֹתָנוּ לָתֶת לָנוּ מום אֶת הָאָרֶץ
אֲשֶׁר נִשְׁבַּע לַאֲבֹתֵינוּ:

*In every generation, one must regard himself as if he personally had gone out of Egypt, as it is says: "And you shall tell your son on that day: 'It was because of this that Hashem did for me when I went out of Egypt.' It was not only our fathers whom the Holy One redeemed from slavery; we, too, were redeemed with them, as it is written: "It brought us out of there in order to take us to and give us the land which He had promised to our fathers."*

### L'FICHACH

*Therefore we must thank God.* God does not need our thanks. To give "thanks" to God is to give our support and care to others in need. The phrase *thank God* actually refers to the spark of God within everyone. "Thank God" refers to people, not the Creator. When we take the time to look after others, God looks after us.

We cover the Matzah and lift the cup while the following is recited:

לְפִיכָךְ אֲנַחְנוּ וַיָּבִים לְהוֹדוֹת לְהַלֵּל לכה לְשַׁבֵּחַ לְפָאֵר
לְרוֹמֵם לְהַדֵּר לְנַצֵּחַ לְבָרֵךְ לְעַלֵּה וּלְקַלֵּס לְמִי שֶׁעָשָׂה
לַאֲבוֹתֵינוּ וְלָנוּ מום אֶת כָּל ילי הַנִּסִּים הָאֵלּוּ. הוֹצִיאָנוּ
מֵעַבְדוּת לְחֵרוּת, מִיָּגוֹן לְשִׂמְחָה, וּמֵאֵבֶל לְיוֹם נגד, ז טוֹב וחל,
וּמֵאֲפֵלָה לְאוֹר ה גָּדוֹל וּמִשַּׁעְבּוּד לִגְאֻלָּה. וְנֹאמַר לְפָנָיו
שִׁירָה וַדְשָׁה הַלְלוּיָהּ מום:

*Therefore, we must thank, praise, pay tribute, glorify, exalt, honor, bless, extol, and acclaim It which performed all these miracles for our fathers and for us all those miracles. Brought us forth from slavery to freedom, from grief to joy, from mourning to festivity, from darkness to great light, and from servitude to redemption. Let us, therefore, recite a new song before Him – Halleluyah!*

### HALLELUYAH

*God lifts me up from dust.* The significance of this verse is the ability for positive change to occur at any moment. No matter how difficult a situation may be, no matter what bind we find ourselves in, the Light of the Creator can repair it all in a moment. The first step is letting go of our egos, which constantly whisper those regretful words to us: "I'm in control." If we tune out those whispers and maintain total certainty that the Light can dramatically alter our situation instantly, we will ignite the power of this connection.

We lower the cup and uncover the Matzah

### CHESED

הַלְלוּיָהּ מוּם הַלְלוּ עַבְדֵי יְהֹוָאדְנָיאהדונהי הַלְלוּ אֶת שֵׁם

יְהֹוָאדְנָיאהדונהי: יְהִי שֵׁם יְהֹוָאדְנָיאהדונהי מְבֹרָךְ רפיז מֵעַתָּה וְעַד

עוֹלָם: מִמִּזְרַח שֶׁמֶשׁ עַד מְבוֹאוֹ מְהֻלָּל שֵׁם יְהֹוָאדְנָיאהדונהי:

רָם עַל כָּל יליּ גּוֹיִם יְהֹוָאדְנָיאהדונהי עַל הַשָּׁמַיִם ייפ טל כְּבוֹדוֹ:

מִי יליּ כַּיהֹוָאדְנָיאהדונהי אֱלֹהֵינוּ ילה הַמַּגְבִּיהִי לָשָׁבֶת: הַמַּשְׁפִּילִי

לִרְאוֹת בַּשָּׁמַיִם ייפ טל וּבָאָרֶץ: מְקִימִי מֵעָפָר דָּל מֵאַשְׁפֹּת

יָרִים אֶבְיוֹן: לְהוֹשִׁיבִי עִם נְדִיבִים עִם נְדִיבֵי עַמּוֹ: מוֹשִׁיבִי

עֲקֶרֶת הַבַּיִת בלף ראה אֵם ייהך הַבָּנִים שְׂמֵחָה הַלְלוּיָהּ מוּם:

*Halleluyah! Praise, you servants of Hashem, praise the Name of Hashem. Blessed be the Name of Hashem from now to eternity. From sunrise till sunset, Hashem's name is praised. High above all nations is Hashem; Its glory is all over the heavens. Who is like Hashem, our God, highly enthroned, yet looks down upon the heaven and the earth? He raises the destitute from the dust, from the trash heaps He lifts the needy – to seat them with nobles, with nobles of His people. He settles down the barren housewife (the Shechinah), and turns Her into a happy mother of sons. Halleluyah!*

### BTZET IRAEL

*Yehuda was holy.* Yehuda refers to the head of the Tribe of Yehuda, a man named Nachshon. He was the first person to demonstrate complete certainty when he entered the Red Sea.[44]

---

44. When Moshe outstretched his arms and his staff to part the Red Sea, the waters didn't move. Not one single water molecule budged an inch. To activate this miracle of nature, the Israelites were forced to activate their own miracle of human nature. That was left to Nachshon, who waded into the water with total certainty. He overcame his reactive fears and doubts and continued into the water until it reached his nostrils, whereupon it rushed into his throat and began choking him. At the precise moment of his choke, Satan attempted to bombard him with fear and uncertainty. But Nachshon didn't waiver. A split second later, he was breathing fresh air as the waters of the Red Sea climbed

## GVURAH

בְּצֵאת יִשְׂרָאֵל מִמִּצְרָיִם מֵי־ בֵּית ־ בפ ראה יַעֲקֹב מֵעַם לֹעֵז:

הָיְתָה יְהוּדָה לְקָדְשׁוֹ יִשְׂרָאֵל מַמְשְׁלוֹתָיו: הַיָּם ילי רָאָה ראה

וַיָּנֹס הַיַּרְדֵּן יִסֹּב לְאָחוֹר: הֶהָרִים רָקְדוּ כְאֵילִים גְּבָעוֹת

כִּבְנֵי צֹאן: מַה מ״ה לְּךָ הַיָּם ילי כִּי תָנוּס הַיַּרְדֵּן תִּסֹּב לְאָחוֹר:

הֶהָרִים תִּרְקְדוּ כְאֵילִים גְּבָעוֹת כִּבְנֵי צֹאן: מִלִּפְנֵי אָדוֹן אני

וּחוּלִי אָרֶץ מִלִּפְנֵי אֱלוֹהַּ אֱלוֹהַ מ״ב יַעֲקֹב: הַהֹפְכִי הַצּוּר אֲגַם

מַיִם וַחַלָּמִישׁ לְמַעְיְנוֹ מָיִם:

*When Israel went forth from Egypt, Jacob's household (went forth) from a people of alien tongue (Egypt),*
*Yehudah became sanctuary, and Israel became governing. The sea saw and fled, the Jordan (river) turned*
*backward. The mountains skipped like rams and the hills like young lambs.What ails you, O sea that you*
*flee? O Jordan that you turn backward? O mountains that you skip like rams? O hills, like young lambs?*
*Before the Lord tremble, O earth, before the God of Jacob, which turns the rock into a lake of water, flint*
*into a flowing fountain.*

### THE BLESSING – REDEEMER OF ISRAEL

The word *G'aal,* which means "redeemer," can be rearranged to spell out the word *Keter,* which means "seed." Keter is the first Sfirot.[45] We are given the ability to seek out the root cause and seed level of all the negative events that transpire in our lives so that we can address and fix the *cause* in order to remove their chaotic effects in our life. We achieve this through the power of Keter, the seed level of the entire cosmos.

### We cover the Matzah and raise our cup of wine

בָּרוּךְ אַתָּה יְהֹוָהאדנ־יאהדונהי אֱלֹהֵינוּ ילה מֶלֶךְ הָעוֹלָם, אֲשֶׁר

גְּאָלָנוּ וְגָאַל אֶת אֲבוֹתֵינוּ מִמִּצְרַיִם מצר, וְהִגִּיעָנוּ הַלַּיְלָה הַזֶּה מלה

הַזֶּה והו לֶאֱכָל בּוֹ מַצָּה וּמָרוֹר.

*Blessed is Hashem, our God, King of the universe, which redeemed us and redeemed our fathers from Egypt*
*and brought us to this night to eat Matzah and horseradish.*

---

toward the heavens. Even when miracles are supposed to happen, the slightest doubt can prevent them from occurring.

45. Ten Sfirot are the dimensions that separate our world from the Endless World. Keter is the highest Sfirah, closest to the Endless World. Keter is the source of all the thoughts, imagination, feelings, knowledge, and creativity that occurs in our physical world.

כֵּן יְהֹוָ‏ה<sup>אדני אהדונהי</sup> אֱלֹהֵינוּ <sup>יה</sup> וֵאלֹהֵי <sup>לכב</sup> אֲבוֹתֵינוּ יַגִּיעֵנוּ לְמוֹעֲדִים וְלִרְגָלִים אֲחֵרִים הַבָּאִים לִקְרָאתֵנוּ לְשָׁלוֹם, שְׂמֵחִים בְּבִנְיַן עִירֶךָ, וְשָׂשִׂים בַּעֲבוֹדָתֶךָ, וְנֹאכַל שָׁם מִן הַזְּבָחִים וּמִן הַפְּסָחִים (במוצ״ש אומרים: מִן הַפְּסָחִים וּמִן הַזְּבָחִים) אֲשֶׁר יַגִּיעַ דָּמָם עַל קִיר מִזְבַּחֲךָ לְרָצוֹן <sup>מהש</sup> וְנוֹדֶה לְךָ שִׁיר חָדָשׁ <sup>יב הויות</sup> עַל גְּאֻלָּתֵנוּ וְעַל פְּדוּת נַפְשֵׁנוּ: בָּרוּךְ אַתָּה יְהֹוָה<sup>אדני אהדונהי</sup> גָּאַל יִשְׂרָאֵל:

*In a similar manner, Hashem, our God and the God of our fathers, will enable us to reach in the future other festivals and holidays – in peace, gladdened in the rebuilding of Your city (Jerusalem), joyful at Your service. There we shall eat of the offerings and Passover sacrifices (on Shabbat we say: of the Passover sacrifices and offerings) whose blood will gain the sides of Your altar for gracious acceptance. We shall then thank You by singing a new song of praise, for our redemption and for the liberation of our soul. Blessed are You, Hashem, which has redeemed Israel.*

## L'SHEM YICHUD

L'shem Yichud acts as a spark plug that activates our desire to connect to spiritual energy. It also serves as a preparation process, readying us for the tremendous forces streaming into our world and into our life.

לְשֵׁם יִחוּד קוּדְשָׁא בְּרִיךְ הוּא וּשְׁכִינְתֵּיהּ בִּדְחִילוּ וּרְחִימוּ וּרְחִימוּ וּדְחִילוּ לְיַחֲדָא שֵׁם יוֹד קֵי בְּוָאו קֵי בְּיִחוּדָא שְׁלִים <sup>יהוה</sup> בְּשֵׁם כָּל <sup>יל</sup> יִשְׂרָאֵל, הִנְנִי מוּכָן וּמְזוּמָּן לְקַיֵּים מִצְוַת כּוֹס <sup>מוה</sup> שֵׁנִי שֶׁל אַרְבַּע כּוֹסוֹת, וִיהִי נֹעַם אֲדֹנָי אֱלֹהֵינוּ <sup>יל</sup> עָלֵינוּ וּמַעֲשֵׂה יָדֵינוּ כּוֹנְנָה עָלֵינוּ וּמַעֲשֵׂה יָדֵינוּ כּוֹנְנֵהוּ:

*For the sake of unifying The Holy One, blessed be It, and Its Shechinah, with fear and mercy, and with mercy and fear, to unify the name of Yud Key with Vav Key completely, in the name of all Israel, I am ready and willing to apply the connection of Second Cup out of Four Cups, and may the pleasantness of Hashem, our God, be upon us, and establish the action of our hands upon us and establish the action of our hands.*

בָּרוּךְ אַתָּה יְהֹוָﬡﬡﬡﬡ אֱלֹהֵינוּ ﬡﬡ מֶלֶךְ הָעוֹלָם
בּוֹרֵא פְּרִי הַגָּפֶן:

*Blessed are You, Hashem, our God, King of the universe, Who creates the fruit of the vine.*

We drink while leaning to the left.

### STAGE SIX: RACHTZA
### NTLAT YADIEM: WASHING OF THE HANDS

During the night, many negative forces latch onto our hands while we sleep. Our hands are like magnets that attract these forces because hands carry out many of our negative actions in our daily lives, and they are the culprits that manifest the negative thoughts that reside in our hearts and minds. According to Kabbalah, the negative thought is the cause of negative behavior, and the hands are the effect that manifests them. The Kabbalists also teach us that positive energy connects to the cause and seed level of reality, but negativity always connects to the effect. By washing our hands each morning, we accomplish two important objectives:

1. We cleanse and wash away all negative forces that cling to our hands.

2. We connect ourselves to the cause and seed level of reality (positivity) and not just the effect.

This duty helps us achieve a more positive and fulfilling day.

We receive another important benefit when we invoke this blessing. Inside the actual words we find a remarkable code. The last three words are *Al Ntilat Yadiem*. The first letter from each of these three words spells *Anee* עֲנִי, Hebrew for "a poor person." When you take the last letters of these three words, *Lamed* ל, *Taf* ת, and *Mem* ם, they have the same numerical value as the word *Ashir* עָשִׁיר. In English, *Ashir* means "a rich person." By washing our hands each morning and preventing negative energy from attaching itself to us all day long, we begin to uproot ourselves from the level of *Anee* (poor) and connect ourselves to the energy of *Ashir* (rich).[46]

Before we recite the blessing, we go to the sink and pour a cup of water over our right hand and then our left hand. We do this twice on each hand.

בָּרוּךְ אַתָּה אל יְהֹוָﬡﬡﬡﬡ רחום וחנון

*Blessed are you, Hashem,*

---

46. "Rich" refers not only to financial sustenance, but also to the concept of being rich with a close and loving family, rich with health, or living a life filled with richness of meaning. The blessing will be directed wherever we need the rich energy.

אֱלֹהֵינוּ ילה ארך מֶלֶךְ אפים הָעוֹלָם ורב חסד אֲשֶׁר ואמת קִדְּשָׁנוּ נצר

חסד בְּמִצְוֹתָיו לאלפים וְצִוָּנוּ נשא עון עַל ופש נְטִילַת וחטאה לְיָדִים ונקה: ידים

*our God, King of the universe, which has sanctified us by His connections and connected us by the washing of the hands.*

### STAGE SEVEN: MOTZI

# מוֹצִיא מַצָּה

Before the actual breaking of bread, we should pray for sustenance. The numerical value of *Hamotzee, L'chem, Meen Ha'aretz* – the blessing over the bread – equals the same value as *Pei Aleph Yod* פאי, *Samech Aleph Lamed* סאל and *Chet Taf final Caf* – חתך three Kabbalistic meditations for creating sustenance and prosperity. Even as we eat, we should pray for sustenance with the realization that nothing is ours. All good fortune emanates from the Light. This awareness helps intensify our prayers.

### STAGE EIGHT: MATZAH

Matzah is the only type of bread that requires a special blessing. Bread is the only food with a dual nature. We eat bread during the year, tapping all of its positive energy. But we cannot eat bread during Passover because of its potentially hazardous effects on our spiritual character and nature.[47]

This dual aspect to bread is mirrored in our behavior. Sometimes we need to activate and use our *desire to receive* (signified by bread) in situations where we are truly lacking self-esteem, ambition, and self-confidence. This blessing helps give us balance and insight as to when to apply our *desire to receive* and when not to. Actions are either positive or negative. But desires and thoughts are gray. Sometimes they occur to test us so that we can overcome them. There are times when we have to be angry toward the negativity of the world to change it. If we are not angry or deeply concerned about the ills of the world, we can never be motivated to help improve the lives of others. Using our internal desires is like stepping on the accelerator pedal in a car. We step on the gas when we need to pick up speed. Once we're moving, we ease up and take our foot off the gas. Likewise, we can use our *desire to receive* to motivate us to action, but once we are moving, we must shut down our egos (signified by the Matzah) and transform them into desires to share. Granted, this is a tough balancing act, but it is one that is made easier through this powerful connection.

---

47. One of the reasons we abstain from bread during Passover, why we cannot even have one crumb in our home, is due to the overwhelming infusion of energy bread transmits. On Passover, this infusion reaches ultra-high levels. Consider this example: A person drives a car at 30 mph. If you roll down the window in the car, the air-pressure change is so minimal, you can still control the vehicle without any trouble. If, however, you were flying in a Concorde jet at the speed of sound, the tiniest crack in a window will set the jet careening out of control. Passover is like flying at the speed of light. That's how intense the Light of freedom is. Even the tiniest speck of bread in your system will send you and your reactive behavior on a wild collision course with chaos throughout the year.

### L'SHEM YICHUD

L'shem Yichud acts as a spark plug that activates our desire to connect to spiritual energy. It also serves as a preparation process, readying us for the tremendous forces streaming into our world and into our life.

We raise all three Matzah on the Seder plate while we recite the following:

לְשֵׁם יִחוּד קוּדְשָׁא בְּרִיך הוּא וּשְׁכִינְתֵּיה בִּדְחִילוּ וּרְחִימוּ

וּרְחִימוּ וּדְחִילוּ לְיַחֲדָא לְיַחֲדָא שֵׁם יוּד קֵי בְּוָאו קֵי בְּיִחוּדָא שְׁלִים

יהה בְּשֵׁם כָּל יֹה יִשְׂרָאֵל, הִנְנִי מוּכָן וּמְזוּמָן לְקַיֵּם מִצְוַת

אֲכִילַת מַצָּה וִיהִי נֹעַם אֲדֹנָי אֱלֹהֵינוּ יֹה עָלֵינוּ וּמַעֲשֵׂה

יָדֵינוּ כּוֹנְנָה עָלֵינוּ וּמַעֲשֵׂה יָדֵינוּ כּוֹנְנֵהוּ:

*For the sake of unifying The Holy One, blessed be It, and Its Shechinah, with fear and mercy, and with mercy and fear, to unify the name of Yud Key with Vav Key completely, in the name of all Israel, I am ready and willing to apply the connection of eating Matzah, and may the pleasantness of Hashem, our God, be upon us, and establish the action of our hands upon us and establish the action of our hands.*

בָּרוּך אַתָּה יְהֹוָאהדונהי אֱלֹהֵינוּ יֹה מֶלֶךְ הָעוֹלָם

הַמּוֹצִיא לֶחֶם מִן הָאָרֶץ:

*Blessed are You, Hashem, our God, King of the universe, Who brings forth bread from the earth.*

We put down the bottom Matzah, break a piece from each of the other two Matzah, and recite the following blessing:

בָּרוּך אַתָּה יְהֹוָאהדונהי אֱלֹהֵינוּ יֹה מֶלֶךְ הָעוֹלָם אֲשֶׁר

קִדְּשָׁנוּ בְּמִצְוֹתָיו וְצִוָּנוּ עַל אֲכִילַת מַצָּה:

*Blessed are You, Hashem, our God, King of the universe, Who has sanctified us by His connections, and connected us to eat Matzah.*

### STAGE NINE: MAROR

מָרוֹר

Maror is the highest yet most difficult connection on Pesach. Maror has the same numerical value as the word *death*. For us to reach the state of immortality, we must taste death. By slowly chewing the Maror and embracing the intense pain it generates, we can proactively taste death and therefore gradually remove the force of death from our own lives.[48] Each chew of the Maror brings us another step closer to genuine immortality.

While we are choking on the Maror, we need to retain this consciousness. Our objective is to give up a little comfort now, for the moment, to achieve infinite fulfillment and lasting comfort forever. Too often we settle for a little comfort now and end up paying for it with a lot of chaos and pain later on.

לְשֵׁם יִחוּד קוּדְשָׁא בְּרִיךְ הוּא וּשְׁכִינְתֵּיהּ בִּדְחִילוּ וּרְחִימוּ

וּרְחִימוּ וּדְחִילוּ לְיַחֲדָא שֵׁם יוּד קֵי בְּוָאו קֵי בְּיִחוּדָא

שְׁלִים יהוה בְּשֵׁם כָּל יִשְׂרָאֵל, הִנְנִי מוּכָן וּמְזוּמָן לְקַיֵּם

מִצְוַת אֲכִילַת מָרוֹר וִיהִי נֹעַם אֲדֹנָי אֱלֹהֵינוּ עָלֵינוּ

וּמַעֲשֵׂה יָדֵינוּ כּוֹנְנָה עָלֵינוּ וּמַעֲשֵׂה יָדֵינוּ כּוֹנְנֵהוּ:

*For the sake of unifying The Holy One, blessed be It, and Its Shechinah, with fear and mercy, and with mercy and fear, to unify the name of Yud Key with Vav Key completely, in the name of all Israel, I am ready and willing to apply the connection of eating maror, and may the pleasantness of Hashem, our God, be upon us, and establish the action of our hands upon us and establish the action of our hands.*

We take the Maror, dip it in the fruit blend, and eat it without leaning

בָּרוּךְ אַתָּה יְהֹוָה אֱלֹהֵינוּ מֶלֶךְ הָעוֹלָם אֲשֶׁר

קִדְּשָׁנוּ בְּמִצְוֹתָיו וְצִוָּנוּ עַל אֲכִילַת מָרוֹר:

*Blessed are You, Hashem, our God, King of the universe, Who has sanctified us by His connections, and connected us to eat horseradish.*

### STAGE TEN: KORECH

כּוֹרֵךְ:

The purpose behind the connection to Korech is to elevate us above the stars and the signs of the zodiac. This is one reason why the Aries – the Ram – was the choice for the sacrifice at the temple on Pesach. Aries is the first sign, the seed, and this is where all the control is. It is also one of the most difficult signs, as any Aries can attest to. If we can go above Aries, we can overcome all obstacles and negative influences. Therefore, the great

---

48. The force of death is not limited to the physical body. Death can also strike at a business, in a marriage, or any kind of relationship.

sage Hillel used the power of Pesach (the Aries), Matza, and Maror to rise above the negative influences of the 12 constellations.

We take the Maror, spread it on a Matzah, and eat them together, leaning to the left, without a blessing. Prior to this we recite the following:

זֵכֶר לְמִקְדָּשׁ כְּהִלֵּל. כֵּן עָשָׂה הִלֵּל. בִּזְמַן שֶׁבֵּית ב"פ ראה

הַמִּקְדָּשׁ הָיָה יהה קַיָם הָיָה יהה כּוֹרֵךְ פֶּסַח מַצָּה וּמָרוֹר

וְאוֹכֵל בְּיַחַד לְקַיֵם מַה מה שֶׁנֶּאֱמַר עַל מַצּוֹת וּמְרֹרִים

יֹאכְלֻהוּ:

*In remembrance of the temple, we do as Hilel did in temple times: he would make a sandwich of Passover offering and horseradish in a Matzah bread and eat them together in order to fulfill what is written in the Torah: "They shall eat it with Matzah and bitter herbs."*

### STAGE ELEVEN: SHULCHAN ORECH

שֻׁלְחָן עוֹרֵךְ:

This next phase of eating the meal appears to play directly to our *desire to receive for the self alone.* Except after all that we have accomplished during our Seder, this is not the case. We are not living to eat, as many people do, but eating to live. We partake of the meal to gain strength to continue on in our spiritual work. Eating is not just for physical gratification. Everything we do can have a spiritual dimension to it simply by having the consciousness and intent to use our physical connections to serve a higher spiritual purpose.

We dine as much as necessary in honor of the holiday.

It is customary to eat an egg.

### STAGE TWELVE: TZAFUN

צָפוּן

*The eating of the Afikoman. Tzafun* means "whatever is hidden is now revealed." There is a Torah story in which Ya'akov goes to his father, Isaac, to receive a blessing. He brings with him a sacrifice for Pesach, which today is represented by our *Afikoman.* When Ya'akov walked into his father's room, the Torah tells us that he could smell the Garden of Eden. After Ya'akov brought the sacrifice, he received the blessing from his father.

How does this story relate to our life? We know that the power of the *Afikoman* is equal to the sacrifices that occurred in ancient times. The numerical value of *Afikoman* is *trickery or deception*. This connects to Ya'akov, who used deception against his evil brother, Esau. Yitzchak originally wanted to give the blessing to Esau, but Ya'akov wore his brother's clothes, fooled his father, and received the blessing instead.

This gives us a clue as to the significance behind the hiding of the *Afikoman*. This action connects us to the sacrifice and deception efforts of Ya'akov so that we can deceive the Satan and remove him from our life. We can now taste from the Garden of Eden (signified by Ya'akov) as opposed to tasting from the fires of Hell (signified by Esau).

We take the Matzah kept for Afikoman, in remembrance of the Passover offering, to be eaten after one is full. We eat it while leaning to the left and recite the following:

### L'SHEM YICHUD

L'shem Yichud acts as a spark plug that activates our desire to connect to spiritual energy. It also serves as a preparation process, readying us for the tremendous forces being transmitted by the Matzah.

לְשֵׁם יִוזוּד קוּדְשָׁא בְּרִיךְ הוּא וּשְׁכִינְתֵּיהּ בִּדְוזִילוּ וּרְוזֹימוּ

וּרְוזֹימוּ וּדְוזִילוּ לְיַוְזִדָא שֵׁם יוּד קֵי בְּוָאו קֵי בְּיִוזוּדָא

שְׁלִים יהוה בְּשֵׁם כָּל יִשְׂרָאֵל, הִנְּנִי מוּכָן וּמְזוּמָן לְקַיֵּם

מִצְוַת אֲכִילַת אֲפִיקוֹמָן. וִיהִי נֹעַם אֲדֹנָי אֱלֹהֵינוּ עָלֵינוּ

וּמַעֲשֵׂה יָדֵינוּ כּוֹנְנָה עָלֵינוּ וּמַעֲשֵׂה יָדֵינוּ כּוֹנְנֵהוּ:

*For the sake of unifying The Holy One, blessed be It, and Its Shechinah, with fear and mercy, and with mercy and fear, to unify the name of Yud Key with Vav Key completely, in the name of all Israel, I am ready and willing to apply the connection of eating Afikoman, and may the pleasantness of Hashem, our God, be upon us, and establish the action of our hands upon us and establish the action of our hands.*

### STAGE THIRTEEN: BARECH

בָּרֵךְ

L'shem Yichud acts as a spark plug that activates our desire to connect to spiritual energy. It also serves as a preparation process, readying us for the tremendous forces transmitted by the *Birkat HaMazon*.

*Birkat HaMazon* elevates actual sparks of Light concealed inside the food we eat and connects it to the Upper Worlds. It removes the physical aspect of the meal (temporary energy), leaving us with the spiritual sustenance that is eternal and everlasting.

We have four blessings inside the *Birkat HaMazon*, connecting us to four Upper Worlds in the spiritual atmosphere. The names of these four worlds are Atzilut, Briah, Yetzirah, and Asiyah. These four worlds are part of the ten dimensions of our universe.

The leader of the Seder now gathers all our efforts and energy into one collective force and elevates it into the Upper Worlds as he launches the *Birkat HaMazon*.

We pour the third cup and recite the following blessing over the food:

לְשֵׁם יְחוּד קוּדְשָׁא בְּרִיךְ הוּא וּשְׁכִינְתֵּיהּ בִּדְחִילוּ וּרְחִימוּ

וּרְחִימוּ וּדְחִילוּ לְיַחֲדָא שֵׁם יוּד קֵי בְּוָאו קֵי בְּיִחוּדָא

שְׁלִים יהוה בְּשֵׁם כָּל יִשְׂרָאֵל, הִנְנִי מוּכָן וּמְזוּמָן לְקַיֵּם

מִצְוַת עֲשֵׂה שֶׁל בִּרְכַּת הַמָּזוֹן, שֶׁנֶּאֱמַר וְאָכַלְתָּ וְשָׂבָעְתָּ

וּבֵרַכְתָּ אֶת יְהֹוָהאדני את אלהיך יהוה עַל הָאָרֶץ הַטּבָה אבא

אֲשֶׁר נָתַן לָךְ, וִיהִי נֹעַם אֲדֹנָי אֱלֹהֵינוּ יהוה עָלֵינוּ וּמַעֲשֵׂה יָדֵינוּ

כּוֹנְנָה עָלֵינוּ וּמַעֲשֵׂה יָדֵינוּ כּוֹנְנֵהוּ:

*For the sake of unifying The Holy One, blessed be It, and Its Shechinah, with fear and mercy, and with mercy and fear, to unify the name of Yud Key with Vav Key completely, in the name of all Israel, I am ready and willing to apply the connection of blessing over the food, as it is written in the Torah: "And you shall eat and you shall be satisfied and you shall bless Hashem, your God, for the good land which It gave you," and may the pleasantness of Hashem, our God, be upon us, and establish the action of our hands upon us and establish the action of our hands.*

### SHIR HAMA'ALOT

שִׁיר הַמַּעֲלוֹת בְּשׁוּב יְהֹוָהאדני את שִׁיבַת צִיּוֹן יוסף הָיִינוּ

כְּחֹלְמִים: אָז יִמָּלֵא שְׂחוֹק פִּינוּ וּלְשׁוֹנֵנוּ רִנָּה אָז יֹאמְרוּ בַגּוֹיִם

הִגְדִּיל יְהֹוָהאדני לַעֲשׂוֹת עִם אֵלֶּה: הִגְדִּיל יְהֹוָהאדני

לַעֲשׂוֹת עִמָּנוּ הָיִינוּ שְׂמֵחִים:

*A song of elevation When Hashem will return the captivity of Zion, we will be like dreamers. Then our mouth will be filled with laughter and our tongue with glad song. Then they will declare among the nations, "Hashem has done greatly with these." Hashem has done greatly with us; we were gladdened.*

שׁוּבָה הַזֶּה יְהֹוָ֨הֲדֹנָי אֶת שְׁבִיתֵנוּ כַּאֲפִיקִים בַּנֶּגֶב:
הַזֹּרְעִים בְּדִמְעָה בְּרִנָּה יִקְצֹרוּ: הָלוֹךְ יֵלֵךְ וּבָכֹה נֹשֵׂא
מֶשֶׁךְ הַזָּרַע בֹּא יָבֹא בְרִנָּה נֹשֵׂא אֲלֻמֹּתָיו:

*O Hashem, return our captivity like brooks in the desert. Those who tearfully sow, will reap in glad song. He who bears the measure of seeds walks along weeping, but will return in exultation, a bearer of his sheaves.*

### Leader

הַב לָן וּנְבָרֵךְ

*Gentlemen, let us bless.*

### Others

יְהִי שֵׁם יְהֹוָ֨הֲדֹנָי מְבֹרָךְ מֵעַתָּה וְעַד עוֹלָם:

*Blessed be the name of Hashem from this time and forever.*

### Leader repeats

יְהִי שֵׁם יְהֹוָ֨הֲדֹנָי מְבֹרָךְ מֵעַתָּה וְעַד עוֹלָם:

*Blessed be the name of Hashem from this time and forever*

---

### On Shabbat we add:

וּבִרְשׁוּת שַׁבָּת מַלְכְּתָא

וּבִרְשׁוּת מוֹרַי וְרַבּוֹתַי

*With the permission of Shabbat, the queen, with the permission of my teachers, and with the permission of the distinguished people present.*

---

### Leader

בִּרְשׁוּת מָרָנָן וְרַבּוֹתַי

נְבָרֵךְ (המזמן בעשרה אֱלֹהֵינוּ)

שֶׁאָכַלְנוּ מִשֶּׁלּוֹ:

*With the permission of my teachers and with the permission of distinguished people present* (**If ten men join in the blessing we add** *our God.*) *Let us bless that of Which we have eaten.*

Others

בָּרוּךְ (בעשרה אֱלֹהֵינוּ ילה) שֶׁאָכַלְנוּ מִשֶּׁלּוֹ וּבְטוּבוֹ וָיִינוּ:

*Let us bless (If ten men join in the blessing we add our God.) That of Which we have eaten, and through Which goodness we live.*

Leader repeats

בָּרוּךְ (בעשרה אֱלֹהֵינוּ ילה) שֶׁאָכַלְנוּ מִשֶּׁלּוֹ וּבְטוּבוֹ וָיִינוּ:

*Let us bless (If ten men join in the blessing we add our God.) That of Which we have eaten, and through Which goodness we live.*

בָּרוּךְ הוּא וּבָרוּךְ שְׁמוֹ מהש ע"ה:

*Blessed is He, and blessed is His name.*

### THE FIRST BLESSING - THE WORLD OF ATZILUT/EMANATION

*God gave sustenance to the whole world.* We are now receiving the power of sustenance and prosperity. But there is one requirement: We must understand that whatever we own is merely on loan. All sustenance originates from the Creator. This awareness ensures that we keep our sustenance our entire life, thus avoiding the financial roller coaster that plagues most families. If we believe that we are the architects and providers of our own wealth, we open ourselves up to the Satan and the potential for ups and downs and loss of sustenance.

בָּרוּךְ אַתָּה יְהֹוָהֹאדנּיאהדונהי אֱלֹהֵינוּ ילה מֶלֶךְ הָעוֹלָם, הַזָּן גגד

אֶת הָעוֹלָם כֻּלּוֹ, בְּטוּבוֹ בְּחֵן מווי בְּחֶסֶד ע"ב וּבְרַחֲמִים מצפצ,

הוּא נֹתֵן לֶחֶם לְכָל אדני יה בָּשָׂר כִּי לְעוֹלָם חַסְדּוֹ: וּבְטוּבוֹ

הַגָּדוֹל תָּמִיד ע"ה נתה לֹא חָסַר לָנוּ מום, וְאַל יֶחְסַר לָנוּ מום מום בְּמָזוֹן

לְעוֹלָם וָעֶד, בַּעֲבוּר שְׁמוֹ מהש ע"ה הַגָּדוֹל כִּי הוּא אֵל זָן גגד

וּמְפַרְנֵס לַכֹּל יה אדני וּמֵטִיב לַכֹּל יה אדני, וּמֵכִין מָזוֹן לְכָל יה אדני

בְּרִיּוֹתָיו אֲשֶׁר בָּרָא קנ"א בן כָּאָמוּר.

*Blessed are you, Hashem, our God, King of the universe, Which nourishes the entire world in His goodness — with grace, with kindness, and with mercy. He gives nourishment to all flesh, for His kindness is eternal. And through His great goodness, we have never lacked and shall never lack nourishment, for all eternity. For the sake of His great Name, because He is a God which nourishes and sustains all and benefits all, and He prepares food for all of Its creatures which He created. As it is said:*

### POTEACH ET YADECHA

Opening our hands is our further recognition that the Light is the origin of all lasting prosperity. This action of turning our hands skyward works like a spiritual antenna, drawing the energy of sustenance to our life. The sages teach us that if we miss this specific action, we must repeat the entire blessing over from the beginning.

פּוֹתֵחַ אֶת יָדֶךָ (יְוַדְהִתוּכָה)

*You open your hands*

פאי סאל וזתך

Sustenance through Tithing

וּמַשְׂבִּיעַ וזתך יה אדני וזי רְצוֹן מהשׁ: לְכָל

בָּרוּךְ אַתָּה יְהֹוָאדניאהדונהי הַזָן נגד אֶת הַכֹּל:

*And satisfy the needs of every living thing. Blessed are You, Hashem, Who nourishes all.*

### THE SECOND BLESSING – THE WORLD OF BRIAH/CREATION

The verse states that we are thanking God. But Kabbalah teaches us that an all-powerful Creator does not need our thanks or recognition. In reality, we are arousing a sense of appreciation only because the energy of appreciation works like a security force that protects all our good fortune. Thanking God also means helping and caring for others because each person on the planet possesses a spark of God within. Thanking and recognizing God really means recognizing and appreciating the people sitting beside us.

נוֹדֶה לְּךָ יְהֹוָאדניאהדונהי אֱלֹהֵינוּ יכה עַל שֶׁהִנְחַלְתָּ לַאֲבוֹתֵינוּ,

אֶרֶץ וְחֶמְדָּה הֶ טוֹבָה אכא וּרְחָבָה, וְעַל שֶׁהוֹצֵאתָנוּ

יְהֹוָאדניאהדונהי אֱלֹהֵינוּ יכה מֵאֶרֶץ מִצְרַיִם מצר, וּפְדִיתָנוּ מִבֵּית

עֲבָדִים, בש ראה וְעַל בְּרִיתְךָ שֶׁחָתַמְתָּ בִּבְשָׂרֵנוּ, וְעַל תּוֹרָתְךָ

שֶׁלִמַּדְתָּנוּ, וְעַל חֻקֶּיךָ שֶׁהוֹדַעְתָּנוּ,

*We thank You, Hashem, our God, because You have given to our forefathers as a heritage a desirable, good, and spacious land; because You removed us, Hashem, our God, from the land of Egypt and You redeemed us from the house of bondage; for Your covenant which You sealed in our flesh; for Your Torah which You taught us and for Your statutes which You made known to us;*

וְעַל חַיִּים בּוּה ע״ה וְחֵן מּוּּי וָחֶסֶד ע״ב שֶׁחוֹנַנְתָּנוּ, וְעַל אֲכִילַת מָזוֹן

שָׁאַתָּה זָן גּבּ וּמְפַרְנֵס אוֹתָנוּ תָּמִיד ע״ה נּתּה, בְּכָל לכב יוֹם גּבּ, זַן

וּבְכָל לכב עֵת וּבְכָל לכב שָׁעָה:

*for life, grace, and loving kindness which You granted us; and for the provision of food with which You nourish and sustain us constantly, in every day, in every season, and in every hour.*

וְעַל הַכֹּל יְהֹוָאדנּיאהדוּנּהי אֱלֹהֵינוּ ילה אֲנַחְנוּ מוֹדִים לָךְ מאה,

וּמְבָרְכִים אוֹתָךְ, יִתְבָּרַךְ שִׁמְךָ בְּפִי כָל ילי חַי וַי תָּמִיד ע״ה נּתה

לְעוֹלָם וָעֶד. כַּכָּתוּב: וְאָכַלְתָּ וְשָׂבָעְתָּ וּבֵרַכְתָּ אֶת

יְהֹוָאדנּיאהדוּנּהי אֱלֹהֶיךָ ילה עַל הָאָרֶץ הַטֹּבָה אכא אֲשֶׁר נָתַן לָךְ:

בָּרוּךְ אַתָּה יְהֹוָאדנּיאהדוּנּהי עַל הָאָרֶץ וְעַל הַמָּזוֹן:

*For all, Hashem, our God, we thank You and bless You. May Your Name be blessed by the mouth of all living, continuously for all eternity. As it is written: "And you shall eat, and you shall be satisfied, and you shall bless Hashem, your God, for the good land that It gave you." Blessed are You, Hashem, for the land and for the nourishment.*

### THE THIRD BLESSING – THE WORLD OF YETZIRAH/FORMATION

*Have Mercy on Israel.* The word *Rachem* (mercy) has a numerical value of 248, the same numerical value as the name *Avraham*. Avraham was known for having constant mercy for all people. 248 is also the number of spiritual and physical body parts of an individual. A surefire method for generating healing energy for all the 248 parts of our body is behaving with mercy toward others, as Avraham did. This blessing is our drawbridge to the Upper Worlds, bringing the healing Light to each of our body parts. When we live our lives with mercy[49] toward others, the bridge is down and the energy flows. When we behave otherwise, the bridge is drawn, cutting off the flow of energy.

In this third blessing, we have two connections – one for Shabbat and one for Passover.

רַחֵם אברהם נָא יְהֹוָאדנּיאהדוּנּהי אֱלֹהֵינוּ ילה. עַל יִשְׂרָאֵל עַמֶּךָ,

*Have mercy, please, Hashem, our God, on Israel Your people;*

---

49. An example of acting with mercy is when we do not react immediately when someone hurts or angers us. Wait. Restrict. According to Kabbalah, mercy means "time." We inject time into our emotions so that we don't react impulsively. Waiting creates a space. Light can now fill this space, inspiring us to respond in the correct spiritual manner appropriate for the situation.

וְעַל יְרוּשָׁלַיִם עִירֶךָ, וְעַל צִיּוֹן יוסף מִשְׁכַּן כְּבוֹדֶךָ ב״ק, לכב. וְעַל
מַלְכוּת בֵּית ב״פ ראה דָּוִד מְשִׁיחֶךָ, וְעַל הַבַּיִת ב״פ ראה הַגָּדוֹל
וְהַקָּדוֹשׁ שֶׁנִּקְרָא שִׁמְךָ עָלָיו. אֱלֹהֵינוּ ילה, אָבִינוּ, רְעֵנוּ, זוּנֵנוּ
פַּרְנְסֵנוּ וְכַלְכְּלֵנוּ, וְהַרְוִיחֵנוּ, וְהַרְוַח לָנוּ מום יְהֹוָאדֹנִיאהדונהי
אֱלֹהֵינוּ ילה מְהֵרָה מִכָּל צָרוֹתֵינוּ. וְנָא, אַל תַּצְרִיכֵנוּ
יְהֹוָאדֹנִיאהדונהי אֱלֹהֵינוּ ילה לֹא לִידֵי מַתְּנַת בָּשָׂר וָדָם וְלֹא
לִידֵי הַלְוָאָתָם. כִּי אִם יודר לְיָדְךָ הַמְּלֵאָה, הַפְּתוּחָה,
הַקְּדוֹשָׁה וְהָרְחָבָה, שֶׁלֹּא נֵבוֹשׁ וְלֹא נִכָּלֵם לְעוֹלָם וָעֶד:

*on Jerusalem, Your city; on Zion, the resting place of Your glory; on the monarchy of the house of David, Your anointed; And on the great and holy house upon which Your Name is called. Our God, our father, tend us, nourish us, sustain us, support us, relieve us, Hashem, our God, and grant us speedy relief from all our troubles. And please, Hashem, our God, do not make us needful of gifts of human hands, nor of their loans, but only of Your Hand that is full, open, holy, and generous, so that we shall gain no shame nor insult for ever and ever.*

---

**SHABBAT**
This blessing is additional to the regular one (see next box),

**If Passover lands on Shabbat:**
On Shabbat, to make the connection to the *Birkat HaMazon*, the third blessing correlates to the realm of Zeir Anpin, the dimension and source for all the spiritual Light that flows into our realm.

רְצֵה וְהַחֲלִיצֵנוּ יְהֹוָאדֹנִיאהדונהי אֱלֹהֵינוּ ילה בְּמִצְוֹתֶיךָ
וּבְמִצְוַת יוֹם נגד, ק הַשְּׁבִיעִי, הַשַּׁבָּת הַגָּדוֹל וְהַקָּדוֹשׁ
הַזֶּה וחו. כִּי יוֹם נגד, ק זֶה גָּדוֹל וְקָדוֹשׁ הוּא לְפָנֶיךָ סמ״ב,
לִשְׁבָּת בּוֹ וְלָנוּחַ בּוֹ בְּאַהֲבָה אחד כְּמִצְוַת רְצוֹנֶךָ.

*May Your energy, Hashem, our God, come for our rescue through Your connections and the seventh day connection, this great and holy Shabbat. For this day is great and holy before You to rest and relax on it in love, to connect and be one with Your energy.*

וּבִרְצוֹנְךָ הָנִיחַ לָנוּ מוֹם יְהוָֹואדניאהדונהי אֱלֹהֵינוּ יכה, שֶׁלֹּא

תְהֵא צָרָה מילוי אלהים וְיָגוֹן וַאֲנָחָה בְּיוֹם נגד, ח בִּמְנוּחָתֵנוּ.

וְהַרְאֵנוּ יְהוָֹואדניאהדונהי אֱלֹהֵינוּ יכה בְּנֶחָמַת צִיּוֹן יוסף עִירֶךָ,

וּבְבִנְיַן יְרוּשָׁלַיִם עִיר קָדְשֶׁךָ, כִּי אַתָּה הוּא בַּעַל

הַיְשׁוּעוֹת וּבַעַל הַנֶּחָמוֹת:

*And with Your will, Hashem, our God, relieve us from distress, grief, and lament on the day of our rest. And show us, Hashem, our God, the consolation of Zion, Your city, and the rebuilding of Jerusalem, city of Your holiness, for You are the Master of salvations and Master of consolations.*

## PASSOVER

This connection injects an additional energy force of freedom into the sparks of Light that are already being elevated into the Upper Worlds courtesy of the *Birkat HaMazon*.

אֱלֹהֵינוּ יכה וֵאלֹהֵי לכב אֲבוֹתֵינוּ, יַעֲלֶה וְיָבֹא וְיַגִּיעַ, וְיֵרָאֶה רי"ו

ראה וְיֵרָצֶה וְיִשָּׁמַע, וְיִפָּקֵד וְיִזָּכֵר זִכְרוֹנֵנוּ וּפִקְדוֹנֵנוּ, וְזִכְרוֹן

אֲבוֹתֵינוּ, וְזִכְרוֹן מָשִׁיחַ בֶּן דָּוִד עַבְדֶּךָ פו, וְזִכְרוֹן יְרוּשָׁלַיִם

עִיר עו"י קָדְשֶׁךָ, וְזִכְרוֹן כָּל יכי עַמְּךָ בֵּית יִשְׂרָאֵל לְפָנֶיךָ

לִפְלֵיטָה לְטוֹבָה אכא, לְחֵן מזו וּלְחֶסֶד ע"ב וּלְרַחֲמִים לְחַיִּים בינה

עה טוֹבִים וּלְשָׁלוֹם. בְּיוֹם נגד, ח חַג הַמַּצּוֹת הַזֶּה והו. זָכְרֵנוּ

יְהוָֹואדניאהדונהי אֱלֹהֵינוּ יכה בּוֹ לְטוֹבָה אכא. וּפָקְדֵנוּ בוֹ לִבְרָכָה.

*Our God and the God of our forefathers, may there rise, come, reach, be noted, be favored, be heard, be considered, and be remembered the remembrance of our forefathers; the remembrance of Messiah, son of David, Your servant; the remembrance of Jerusalem, the city of Your holiness; the remembrance of Your entire people, the house of Israel – before You; for deliverance, for goodness, for grace, for kindness, and for compassion, for good life and for peace, on this Day of Matzot Festival. Remember us on it, Hashem, our God, for goodness; consider us on it for blessing;*

וְהוֹשִׁיעֵנוּ בּוֹ לְחַיִּים בּיה ע״ה טוֹבִים. וּבְדָבָר רֵאה יְשׁוּעָה
וְרַחֲמִים. חוּס וְחָנֵּנוּ, וַחֲמוֹל וְרַחֵם אברהם עָלֵינוּ וְהוֹשִׁיעֵנוּ, כִּי
אֵלֶיךָ עֵינֵינוּ. כִּי אֵל מֶלֶךְ חַנּוּן וְרַחוּם אָתָּה:

*and help us on it for good life. And in the matter of salvation and compassion, pity, pardon us, have mercy upon us, and save us; for our eyes are turned to You, because – You are God, gracious and compassionate King.*

## UVNEH YRUSHALAYIM

The third blessing ends with the verse *Jerusalem will be built with mercy.*

The reason the Temple of Jerusalem was destroyed some 2,000 years ago was due to *Hatred for Reason.* This kind of hatred epitomizes a complete lack of mercy and tolerance between one person and another. The only way the temple will be rebuilt, physically, is through the power *of Love for No Reason* – meaning unconditional mercy and human dignity toward our friends and enemies.

Interestingly, Kabbalah teaches us that the temple already exists spiritually. We can bring it into physical manifestation by virtue of our unconditional love for others. Each year the temple does not appear, it's as though we've destroyed it all over again. It is this destruction that brings about all the chaos in our world.

וּבְנֵה יְרוּשָׁלַיִם עִיר ע״ה הַקֹּדֶשׁ בִּמְהֵרָה בְיָמֵינוּ.
בָּרוּךְ אַתָּה יְהֹוָה אדני אהדונהי בּוֹנֵה ס״ג בְּרַחֲמָיו יְרוּשָׁלָיִם. אָמֵן:

*And rebuild Jerusalem, the holy city, soon in our days. Blessed are You, Hashem, Which rebuilds Jerusalem in His mercy. Amen.*

## THE FOURTH BLESSING – THE WORLD OF ASIYAH/ACTION

*Hatov V'hametiv – All the good that God has done, is doing, and will do for us.* This blessing means that whatever God gives us is what we need and not necessarily what we might want. If we are missing anything in our life, it means we are not supposed to have it. We should always try to receive everything that life can offer us, but we should not allow ourselves to be controlled by the outcome of our efforts to receive. We must learn to fully appreciate and be completely happy with all that we have in the present and not focus our efforts on attaining the next level of success as a condition for our happiness.[50]

---

50. Rav Ashlag, the founder of the Kabbalah Centre in Jerusalem in 1922, revealed a startling disclosure concerning a man's desire in his Kabbalistic treatise *Entrance to the Zohar.* Briefly stated, Rav Ashlag explains that a man begins life with a desire to receive 100 of a commodity. When he attains this 100, the Satan then expands his desire so that he now desires 200. When he attains 200, the Satan expands the desire to 400. When he attains 400, the Satan expands his vessel so that he now desires 800. This expansion continues until the day the man dies. He then leaves this world, sad and frustrated at having fulfilled only half of his desires. When we restrict our *desire to receive for the self alone* and transform it into one of sharing, we become fulfilled completely by the Light. Another way to prevent our desires from inflating out of control is to simply appreciate all that we have right now.

בָּרוּךְ אַתָּה יְהֹוָה<sub>אדני</sub>אהדונהי: אֱלֹהֵינוּ ילה מֶלֶךְ הָעוֹלָם, הָאֵל לאה

אָבִינוּ, מַלְכֵּנוּ, אַדִירֵנוּ, בּוֹרְאֵנוּ, גּוֹאֲלֵנוּ, יוֹצְרֵנוּ, קְדוֹשֵׁנוּ

קְדוֹשׁ יַעֲקֹב, רוֹעֵנוּ רוֹעֵה יִשְׂרָאֵל. הַמֶּלֶךְ הַטּוֹב הו,

וְהַמֵּטִיב לַכֹּל יה אדני, שֶׁבְּכָל לכב יוֹם גנר, ח וָיוֹם גנר, ח הוּא הֵטִיב,

הוּא מֵטִיב, הוּא יֵיטִיב לָנוּ מום, הוּא גְּמָלָנוּ, הוּא גוֹמְלֵנוּ,

הוּא יִגְמְלֵנוּ לָעַד ב"פ ב"ן לְחֵן מזו וּלְחֶסֶד מהי ע"ב וּלְרַחֲמִים

וּלְרֶוַח, הַצָּלָה וְהַצְלָחָה, בְּרָכָה וִישׁוּעָה, נֶחָמָה, פַּרְנָסָה

וְכַלְכָּלָה, וְרַחֲמִים, וְחַיִּים בינה ע"ה וְשָׁלוֹם, וְכָל טוֹב הו, וּמִכָּל

טוּב הו לְעוֹלָם אַל יְחַסְּרֵנוּ.

*Blessed are You, Hashem, our God, King of the universe, the Almighty, our Father, our King, our Sovereign, our Former, our Redeemer, our Creator, our Holy One, Holy One of Jacob, our Shepherd, the Shepherd of Israel, the For every single day It did good, It does good, It will do good to us. King Who is good and Who does good for all. It was bountiful with us, It is bountiful with us, It will forever be bountiful with us – with grace and with kindness and with mercy, with relief, salvation, success, blessing, help, consolation, sustenance, support, mercy, life, peace, and all good; and of all good things, may It never deprive us.*

The leader puts down the cup.

### HARACHAMAN

In these next blessings, we will ask God for everything – health, happiness, sustenance, the final redemption. You name it, we're asking for it.

The Kabbalists ask what the point is in praying for anything. Either God has it in the cards for us to receive, or he doesn't. The reason for asking has to do with ego, which is the only stumbling block to receiving any form of lasting fulfillment. If a person can't admit to himself that he needs God, then he can never receive Light. No matter how many positive actions we do, no matter how smart we are, without admitting and recognizing the need for the Light of the Creator, we can never receive permanent fulfillment. [51]

---

51. Does God need our recognition? Does life have to push us to the breaking point, where we finally cave in and admit we need the Creator? The Kabbalists teach us that we can avoid this scenario by understanding that our denials or doubts concerning the reality of a Creator are really the handiwork of Satan. Satan constantly plants doubt and uncertainty in our minds so that we will believe that we are the orchestrates of our own success. When we admit to this, as well as admitting to all of our faults, we defeat the Satan in one fell swoop.

Now, when you feel the Light afterward, you will come to know God. You will recognize the doubts and uncertainties for what they really are—the influence of Satan. We must always remember that each

הָרַחֲמָן, הוּא יִמְלֹךְ עָלֵינוּ לְעוֹלָם וָעֶד׃

הָרַחֲמָן, הוּא יִתְבָּרֵךְ בַּשָּׁמַיִם טל י'פ וּבָאָרֶץ׃

הָרַחֲמָן, הוּא יִשְׁתַּבַּח י''פ ע''ב לְדוֹר דוֹרִים, וְיִתְפָּאַר בָּנוּ לָעַד

ב''פ ב''ן וּלְנֵצַח נְצָחִים, וְיִתְהַדַּר בָּנוּ לָעַד ב''פ ב''ן וּלְעוֹלְמֵי

עוֹלָמִים׃

הָרַחֲמָן, הוּא יְפַרְנְסֵנוּ בְכָבוֹד בוכו׃

הָרַחֲמָן, הוּא יִשְׁבֹּר עֻלֵּנוּ מֵעַל עלב צַוָּארֵנוּ וְהוּא יוֹלִיכֵנוּ

קוֹמְמִיּוּת לְאַרְצֵנוּ׃

הָרַחֲמָן, הוּא יִשְׁלַח לָנוּ מום בְּרָכָה מְרֻבָּה בַּבַּיִת ב''פ ראה

הַזֶּה וד''ו וְעַל שֻׁלְחָן זֶה שֶׁאָכַלְנוּ עָלָיו׃

הָרַחֲמָן, הוּא יִשְׁלַח לָנוּ מום אֶת אֵלִיָּהוּ לכב הַנָּבִיא זָכוּר יהי אור

לַטּוֹב וד''ו בזזוך, סנדלפון, ערי, וִיבַשֶּׂר לָנוּ מום בְּשׂוֹרוֹת טוֹבוֹת ע''ה

יְשׁוּעוֹת וְנֶחָמוֹת׃

הָרַחֲמָן, הוּא יְבָרֵךְ עסמ''ב אֶת הָרַב רַבִּי מוֹרִי

*The compassionate One! May He reign over us forever. The compassionate One! May He be blessed in heaven and on earth. The compassionate One! May He be praised throughout all generations, may It be glorified through us forever to the ultimate ends, and be honored through us forever and for all eternity. The compassionate One! May He sustain us in honor. The compassionate One! May He break the yoke of oppression from our necks And guide us erect to our land. The compassionate One! May He send us abundant blessing to this house and upon this table at which we have eaten. The compassionate One! May He send us Elijah the Prophet – who is remembered for good – to proclaim to us good tidings, salvations, and consolations. The compassionate One! May He bless the Rav, my teacher,*

time we find it difficult to admit our ugliest of traits or that we need God, it's not you who is feeling those feelings. It is the Satan impressing those feelings into you. Our denial is his way of hiding and concealing himself. The only way to expose and defeat the Satan within is to break the ego, stop the reactive doubts, and admit and ask God for help.

בַּעַל הַבַּיִת בּ״פ ראה הַזֶּה וּהו׳, וְאֶת הָרַבָּנִית מוֹרָתִי בַּעֲלַת

הַבַּיִת בּ״פ ראה הַזֶּה וּהו׳, אוֹתָם וְאֶת בֵּיתָם בּ״פ ראה וְאֶת זַרְעָם

וְאֶת כָּל יל׳ אֲשֶׁר לָהֶם.

הָרַחֲמָן, הוּא יְבָרֵךְ עסמ״ב אוֹתִי וְאֶת אָבִי וְאֶת אִמִּי וְאֶת אִשְׁתִּי וְזַרְעִי

וְאֶת כָּל יל׳ אֲשֶׁר לִי. וְאֶת כָּל יל׳ הַמְּסֻבִּין כָּאן אוֹתָם

וְאֶת בֵּיתָם בּ״פ ראה וְאֶת זַרְעָם וְאֶת כָּל יל׳ אֲשֶׁר לָהֶם אוֹתָנוּ

וְאֶת כָּל יל׳ אֲשֶׁר לָנוּ מוּה, כְּמוֹ שֶׁנִּתְבָּרְכוּ אֲבוֹתֵינוּ אַבְרָהָם

יִצְחָק וזכמה ד״פ ב״ן וְיַעֲקֹב: בַּכֹּל לכב, מִכֹּל, כֹּל יל׳. כֵּן יְבָרֵךְ

עסמ״ב אוֹתָנוּ כֻּלָּנוּ יַחַד, בִּבְרָכָה שְׁלֵמָה, וְנֹאמַר אָמֵן:

*the master of this house, and the Rav's wife, my teacher, the lady of this house: them, their house, their family, and all that is theirs. All our friends, wherever they are: them, their house, their family, and all that is theirs. The compassionate One! (If dining on one's own: May He bless me, (my father and mother,) my wife, my children, and all that is mine.) All the guests here: them, their houses, their families, and all that is theirs, us and all that is ours, just as our forefathers Abraham, Isaac, and Jacob were blessed in everything, from everything, with everything. So may He bless us all together with a perfect blessing, and let us say: Amen!*

בַּמָּרוֹם יְלַמְּדוּ עֲלֵיהֶם וְעָלֵינוּ זְכוּת, שֶׁתְּהֵא לְמִשְׁמֶרֶת

שָׁלוֹם, וְנִשָּׂא בְרָכָה מֵאֵת יְהֹוָה אדני׳, וּצְדָקָה מֵאֱלֹהֵי דמב

יִשְׁעֵנוּ, וְנִמְצָא חֵן מוזי׳ וְשֵׂכֶל טוֹב וּהו׳ בְּעֵינֵי מ״ה ברבוע אֱלֹהִים ילה

וְאָדָם.

*On high, may merit be pleaded upon them and upon us, for a safeguard of peace. May we receive a blessing from Hashem, and favor from the God of our salvation, and find the secrets (of the Torah) and common sense in the eyes of God and man.*

---

**ON SHABBAT**

הָרַחֲמָן, הוּא יַנְחִילֵנוּ יוֹם גגד, ן, שֶׁכֻּלּוֹ שַׁבָּת

*The compassionate One! May He cause us to inherit a day which is completely Shabbat*

וּמְנוּחָה לְחַיֵּי הָעוֹלָמִים.

*and rest for eternal life.*

הָרַחֲמָן, הוּא יַנְחִילֵנוּ יוֹם גם־ה, זן שֶׁכֻּלּוֹ טוֹב והו.

הָרַחֲמָן, הוּא יְזַכֵּנוּ לִימוֹת הַמָּשִׁיחַ וּלְחַיֵּי הָעוֹלָם הַבָּא.

*The compassionate One! May He cause us to inherit a day which is completely good. The compassionate One! May He make us worthy of the days of Messiah and the life of the World to Come (the true world).*

מִגְדוֹל יְשׁוּעוֹת מַלְכּוֹ פי׳ וְעֹשֶׂה חֶסֶד ע״ב לִמְשִׁיחוֹ לְדָוִד וּלְזַרְעוֹ עַד עוֹלָם: עֹשֶׂה שָׁלוֹם בִּמְרוֹמָיו, הוּא יַעֲשֶׂה שָׁלוֹם, עָלֵינוּ וְעַל כָּל ילי יִשְׂרָאֵל, וְאִמְרוּ אָמֵן: יְראוּ אֶת יְהֹוָ אהדניאהדונהי קְדֹשָׁיו, כִּי אֵין מַחְסוֹר לִירֵאָיו: כְּפִירִים רָשׁוּ וְרָעֵבוּ וְדֹרְשֵׁי יְהֹוָ אהדניאהדונהי לֹא יַחְסְרוּ כָל ילי טוֹב והו.

הוֹדוּ אהיה לַיהֹוָ אהדניאהדונהי כִּי טוֹב והו, כִּי לְעוֹלָם חַסְדּוֹ:

*From the greatness of His majestic salvations and kind favors to His anointed, to David and to his descendants forever. The One that makes peace in His heights shall make peace upon us and upon all Israel. Now say: Amen! Fear Hashem, all His holy ones, for there is no deprivation for to the ones who fear him. Young lions may become poor and hungry, but the seekers of Hashem will not lack any good. Thank Hashem, for He is good, for His kindness endures forever.*

### POTEACH ET YADECHA

Opening our hands is our further recognition that the Light is the origin of all lasting prosperity. This action of tuning our hands skyward actually works like a spiritual antenna, drawing the energy of sustenance to our life. The sages teach us that if we miss this specific action, we must repeat the entire blessing over from the beginning.

פּוֹתֵחַ אֶת יָדֶךָ (יוֹהָתוּכָה)

*You open your hands*

פָּאִי סָאל וֹתֶךְ

Sustenance through Tithing

וּמַשְׂבִּיעַ וזתר לְכָל יה אדני וְזֶי רָצוֹן מהש:

*And satisfy the needs of every living thing.*

בָּרוּךְ הַגֶּבֶר אֲשֶׁר יִבְטַח בַּיהֹוָאֲדֹנָיאהדונהי וְהָיָה יהה יהוה
יְהֹוָאֲדֹנָיאהדונהי מִבְטַחוֹ: נַעַר הָיִיתִי גַּם זָקַנְתִּי וְלֹא רָאִיתִי
צַדִּיק נֶעֱזָב וְזַרְעוֹ מְבַקֶּשׁ לָחֶם: יְהֹוָאֲדֹנָיאהדונהי עֹז לְעַמּוֹ יִתֵּן

יְהֹוָאֲדֹנָיאהדונהי יְבָרֵךְ עסמ״ב אֶת עַמּוֹ בַשָּׁלוֹם:

*Blessed is the man that trusts in Hashem, then Hashem will be his security. I was a youth and also have aged, yet I have not seen a righteous man forsaken and his children begging for bread. Hashem will give might to Its people. Hashem will bless Its people with peace.*

### L'SHEM YICHUD

L'shem Yichud acts as a spark plug that activates our desire to connect to spiritual energy. It also serves as a preparation process, readying us for the tremendous forces being transmitted.

לְשֵׁם יִחוּד קוּדְשָׁא בְּרִיךְ הוּא וּשְׁכִינְתֵיהּ בִּדְחִילוּ וּרְחִימוּ
וּרְחִימוּ וּדְחִילוּ לְיַחֲדָא שֵׁם יוּד קֵי בְּוָאו קֵי בְּיִחוּדָא
שְׁלִים יהוה בְּשֵׁם כָּל ילי יִשְׂרָאֵל, הִנְנִי מוּכָן וּמְזוּמָן לְקַיֵּים
מִצְוַת כּוֹס מום שְׁלִישִׁי שֶׁל אַרְבַּע כּוֹסוֹת, וִיהִי נֹעַם אֲדֹנָי
אֱלֹהֵינוּ ילה עָלֵינוּ וּמַעֲשֵׂה יָדֵינוּ כּוֹנְנָה עָלֵינוּ וּמַעֲשֵׂה יָדֵינוּ
כּוֹנְנֵהוּ:

*For the sake of unifying The Holy One, blessed be It, and Its Shechinah, with fear and mercy, and with mercy and fear, to unify the name of Yud Key with Vav Key completely, in the name of all Israel, I am ready and willing to apply the connection of Third Cup out of Four Cups, and may the pleasantness of Hashem, our God, be upon us, and establish the action of our hands upon us and establish the action of our hands.*

### THE THIRD CUP OF WINE – YETZIRAH

There are four cups of wine poured during the course of the Seder. These four cups signify and connect us to the four-letter name of God – the Tetragrammaton[52] – and four Upper Worlds in our spiritual atmosphere. The names of these worlds are Atzilut, Briah, Yetzirah, Asiyah.

We make the blessing on the third cup and drink it while leaning to the left.[53]

בָּרוּךְ אַתָּה יְהֹוָה אֱלֹהֵינוּ מֶלֶךְ הָעוֹלָם

בּוֹרֵא פְּרִי הַגָּפֶן:

*Blessed are You, Hashem, our God, King of the universe, Who creates the fruit of the vine.*

### SHFOCH CHAMATCHA

We fill up the cup of *Eliyahu the prophet.*

We invite *Eliyahu the Prophet* because he is the one who will greet the Messiah when he arrives. *Eliyahu* was chosen because he is the only angel who has a dual function. In this world he is a person. In the Upper Worlds he is an angel. Therefore, he is the bridge to the Upper Worlds for all humanity. For us to achieve the level of being close to God, as the angels are, we have *Eliyahu* as our vehicle. When the Mashiach comes, we will all be like angels, which means we won't need teachers or angels any longer. Everyone will know how to connect to God at the highest possible level.

There seems to be inconsistency concerning the concept of free will and angels. Most of us are taught that only man has free will. Yet it is also written that some angels have free will, which explains why some angels have been known to commit sin.

Kabbalah explains the discrepancy. Kabbalah contends that angels do not have true free will because they are so close to the Light of the Creator. This extreme nearness makes it so clear and simple for them not to commit sin for they are privy to the law of cause and effect. They foresee the consequences of any negative action. They know that any wrongdoing will disconnect them from the blazing Light of the Creator. Therefore, their decisions to choose positive actions are easy for them to make. We, on the other hand, are in a world of darkness, on a much lower level than the angels. We do not feel the Light of God as easily. We do not realize that chaos is an absence of the Creator's Light. Consequently, we are attracted to the *desire to receive for the self alone* – reactive behavior. Elijah the Prophet gives us a heightened awareness and sensitivity to feel the potential of God's Light so that we will be motivated to transform our actions.

The reason *Eliyahu* comes before the Messiah in this story is to teach us that we must first learn to feel the Light and presence God in our lives, before the personal and global

---

52. The Tetragrammaton is a powerful combination of Hebrew letters that literally transmits the spiritual forces of the Upper World into our physical existence. The four letters of the Tetragrammaton are יהוה.

53. We've learned that there are three forces imbedded into the cosmos—Right Column desire to share; Left Column desire to receive; and Central Column, free will to choose and transform our desires. These three forces express themselves in the human body as follows: Left arm, desire to receive; right arm, desire to share; head, free will to choose and control these desires. We lean on our left side as a way to subjugate and take control of the selfish *desire to receive for oneself alone*. Every physical action in our world has a corresponding effect on the Upper Worlds.

Mashiach[54] can arrive.

We now open the door to invite him to our seder, and recite the following:

שְׁפוֹךְ וַזְמָתְךָ אֶל הַגּוֹיִם אֲשֶׁר לֹא יְדָעוּךָ וְעַל מַמְלָכוֹת

אֲשֶׁר בְּשִׁמְךָ לֹא קָרָאוּ: כִּי אָכַל אֶת יַעֲקֹב וְאֶת נָוֵהוּ

הֵשַׁמּוּ: שְׁפֹךְ עֲלֵיהֶם זַעְמֶךָ וַחֲרוֹן אַפְּךָ יַשִּׂיגֵם: תִּרְדֹּף

בְּאַף וְתַשְׁמִידֵם מִתַּחַת שְׁמֵי יְהוָֹהאדנילאהדונהי:

*Pour your wrath upon the nations that do not recognize You and upon kingdoms that do not invoke Your Name. For they have devoured Jacob and turned his habitation into a wilderness. Pour Your anger upon them, and let Your fiery wrath overtake them. Pursue them with wrath, and annihilate them from beneath the heavens of Hashem.*

We close the door.

### STAGE FOURTEEN: HALEL

The Halel connects to Malchut, our physical realm of existence. The numerical value of Halel is the same as the *Lamed, Lamed, Hey* ללה, one of the 72 Names of God.[55] It is also the same numerical value as *Aleph, Daled, Nun, Yud* אדני the name of God that directly correlates and transmits energy into to our physical world.

We pour the fourth cup and complete the Halel.

### TIFERET - LO LANU

*Not for us God, not for us, Do it for your name!* Rav Ashlag teaches us the inner meaning of this verse: Whatever we are able to achieve spiritually, on our own, we still can never truly earn or merit the degree of Light that glimmers inside of us.

Our physical body may not deserve anything in this world, but the Creator also gave us a part of Himself, the spark of Light that sustains our soul and is our essence. This spark of Light is known by the code word *name,* from the verse *Do it for your name!* In reality, we are asking the Creator to give us Light for the Light part of us.

To ensure that God responds to this prayer, we must mirror our request through actions. We do that when we share with others by recognizing the spark of Light within them. Even our worst enemy is imbued with a spark of the Light of God. The more we recognize that, the more blessing and good fortune we receive in our own life.

---

54. There are two levels of Messiah—personal and global. Each person can achieve his own personal Messiah in his life by achieving a complete transformation of character. When enough individuals achieve their own personal Messiah, a critical mass will be met that will produce the global Mashiach bringing total peace, fulfillment, and immortality to the entire world.

55. The 72 Names of God is a formula Moses used to engineer the miracles in Egypt. This formula was concealed inside the holy Zohar for more than 2,000 years. It consists of 72 three-letter sequences encoded inside the story of Exodus in the Torah. Each three-letter sequence gives us a particular power to overcome the numerous negative traits of human nature, in the same way that Moses used this spiritual technology to overpower the laws of mother nature.

לֹא לָנוּ מום יְהֹוָואדנייאהדונהי לֹא לָנוּ מום כִּי לְשִׁמְךָ כִּי לְשִׁמְךָ תֵּן כָּבוֹד עַל

וַחַסְדְּךָ עַל אֲמִתֶּךָ: לָמָּה יֹאמְרוּ הַגּוֹיִם אַיֵּה נָא אֱלֹהֵיהֶם ילה:

וֵאלֹהֵינוּ ילה בַשָּׁמַיִם כֹּל יל אֲשֶׁר וְחָפֵץ עָשָׂה: עֲצַבֵּיהֶם

כֶּסֶף וְזָהָב מַעֲשֵׂה יְדֵי אָדָם: פֶּה מוּם לָהֶם וְלֹא יְדַבֵּרוּ ראה

עֵינַיִם לָהֶם וְלֹא יִרְאוּ: אָזְנַיִם לָהֶם וְלֹא יִשְׁמָעוּ אַף לָהֶם

וְלֹא יְרִיחוּן: יְדֵיהֶם וְלֹא יְמִישׁוּן רַגְלֵיהֶם וְלֹא יְהַלֵּכוּ לֹא

יֶהְגּוּ בִּגְרוֹנָם: כְּמוֹהֶם יִהְיוּ עֹשֵׂיהֶם כֹּל יל אֲשֶׁר בֹּטֵחַ

בָּהֶם: יִשְׂרָאֵל בְּטַח בַּיְהֹוָואדנייאהדונהי עֶזְרָם וּמָגִנָּם הוּא:

בֵּית ב"פ ראה אַהֲרֹן בִּטְחוּ בַיְהֹוָואדנייאהדונהי עֶזְרָם וּמָגִנָּם הוּא:

יִרְאֵי יְהֹוָואדנייאהדונהי בִּטְחוּ בַיְהֹוָואדנייאהדונהי עֶזְרָם וּמָגִנָּם הוּא:

*Not for our sake, Hashem, not for our sake, but for the sake of Your Name give glory, for the sake of Your kindness and Your truth. Why should the nations say: where is their God? Our God is in the Heavens. He formed all that He desired. Their idols are of silver and gold, the work of the hands of man. They have mouths but cannot speak. They have eyes but cannot see. They have noses but cannot smell. Their hands cannot touch, their legs cannot walk. They utter no sounds from their throats. May their makers be like them and whoever trusts in them. Israel, place your trust in Hashem. He is your helper and protector. The House of Aharon, place your trust in Hashem. He is your helper and protector. Those who fear Hashem, place your trust in Hashem. He is your helper and protector. (Psalms 115:1-11)*

## NETZACH - Hashem

***The Heavens were given to God, but the land was given to the people.*** God separated Himself from this world so that we could become creators and express the godliness that is part of all of us. This paragraph gives us the strength to become true creators in our own lives.[56]

יְהֹוָואדנייאהדונהי זְכָרָנוּ יְבָרֵךְ יְבָרֵךְ אֶת בֵּית ב"פ ראה יִשְׂרָאֵל

*Hashem Who remembers us, blesses. He blesses the House of Israel.*

---

56. A tiny candle, glimmering on a blazing sunlit day, has no real worth or value in that setting. But even the darkness of a large stadium must respond to the lighting of one candle. In this realm of darkness, one candle suddenly takes on tremendous value and worth. For this reason, the Light of God was concealed so that our own actions of sharing and creating Light would have value and worth in our lives. This is how we become true creators in our life. When we become creators, we attain a similarity of form as the Creator and oneness is achieved.

יְבָרֵךְ אֶת בֵּית בפּ ראה אַהֲרֹן: יְבָרֵךְ יִרְאֵי יהו∙ה∙אדני∙
הַקְּטַנִּים עִם הַגְּדֹלִים: יֹסֵף יהו∙ה∙אדני∙ עֲלֵיכֶם עֲלֵיכֶם וְעַל
בְּנֵיכֶם: בְּרוּכִים אַתֶּם לַיהו∙ה∙אדני∙ עֹשֵׂה שָׁמַיִם וָאָרֶץ:
הַשָּׁמַיִם שָׁמַיִם לַיהו∙ה∙אדני∙ וְהָאָרֶץ נָתַן לִבְנֵי אָדָם: לֹא
הַמֵּתִים יְהַלְלוּ יָהּ ההה וְלֹא כָּל יל יֹרְדֵי דוּמָה: וַאֲנַחְנוּ נְבָרֵךְ
יָהּ ההה מֵעַתָּה וְעַד עוֹלָם הַלְלוּיָהּ: מזם:

*He blesses the House of Aharon. He blesses those who fear Hashem, the small as well as the great. May Hashem add more upon you. Upon you and upon your children. Blessed are you to Hashem, Creator of Heaven and earth. The Heavens are the Heavens of Hashem, and the earth He gave to mankind. The dead do not praise Hashem, nor do those who descend to the grave. And we will bless God from now and forever, Praise God. (Psalms 115:12-end)*

## HOD - AHAVTI

Rabbi Elimelech, a great Kabbalist who lived about 200 years ago, teaches us that while we pray, the Satan often comes to us to say: "Why are you bothering to stand here and pray? You don't really want to change. It's too difficult. So why bother with all this complicated spiritual work? There's too much to learn, too much to do. You'll never make it. And with all the negative actions you did before, your personal situation is hopeless."

Understand right now that it doesn't matter what we did before. From this moment forward, we can change and transform our nature if we really want to.

This prayer shuts down the Satan's negative and destructive influences.

Every person can change. Everyone has an opening.

*God protects and saves the fools.* Is God really focusing all his efforts on the fools of this world? Not really. The smartest of men make boneheaded mistakes. If we think we really know it all, if our egos tell us that we are brilliant people, then we really are fools and the Light will never reach us. But for those people who can admit that there is always something to learn, no matter how smart we think we are, that person is really saying that he's a fool, in a proactive manner. God will then protect him and take him to even higher levels of fulfillment.

אָהַבְתִּי כִּי יִשְׁמַע יהו∙ה∙אדני∙ אֶת קוֹלִי תַּחֲנוּנָי: כִּי הִטָּה
אָזְנוֹ לִי וּבְיָמַי אֶקְרָא: אֲפָפוּנִי וְחֶבְלֵי מָוֶת וּמְצָרֵי שְׁאוֹל מְצָאוּנִי

*I wanted that Hashem would listen to my voice and to my supplications and turn His Ear towards me and that in my days I would call. Pangs of death have surrounded me and the misery of the grave has found me.*

צָרָה וְיָגוֹן אֶמְצָא: וּבְשֵׁם יְהוָֹ\אדניאהדונהי אֶקְרָא אָנָּה

יְהוָֹ\אדניאהדונהי מַלְּטָה הֵם נַפְשִׁי: חַנּוּן יְהוָֹ\אדניאהדונהי וְצַדִּיק

וֵאלֹהֵינוּ ילה מְרַחֵם אברהם: שֹׁמֵר פְּתָאִים יְהוָֹ\אדניאהדונהי דַּלּוֹתִי

וְלִי יְהוֹשִׁיעַ: שׁוּבִי נַפְשִׁי לִמְנוּחָיְכִי כִּי יְהוָֹ\אדניאהדונהי גָּמַל

עָלָיְכִי: כִּי חִלַּצְתָּ נַפְשִׁי מִמָּוֶת אֶת עֵינִי מִן דִּמְעָה אֶת רַגְלִי

מִדֶּחִי: אֶתְהַלֵּךְ לִפְנֵי יְהוָֹ\אדניאהדונהי בְּאַרְצוֹת הַחַיִּים:

הֶאֱמַנְתִּי כִּי אֲדַבֵּר ראה אֲנִי אני עָנִיתִי מְאֹד: אֲנִי אני אָמַרְתִּי

בְחָפְזִי כָּל ילי הָאָדָם כֹּזֵב:

*I found trouble and sorrow. Then, I called the Name of Hashem: Please, Hashem, rescue my soul. For Hashem is gracious and righteous and our God is merciful. Hashem watches over the simple people. I became destitute and He saved me. My soul return to your peacefulness, for Hashem has dealt kindly with you. For You have salvaged my soul from death and my eyes from tears, and my feet from falling. I shall walk before Hashem in the land of the living. I believed even as I spoke, when I was greatly impoverished, and I said in my haste, all men are treacherous. (Psalms 116:1-11)*

### YESOD - MA

In this paragraph we find the verse *Ana Hashem*. This is the name of a haunting melody that is sung frequently at the Kabbalah Centre. In this verse, we are asking God to give us signs, teachers, directions, and pathways that will lead us to the Light. We are requesting God to be a true spiritual master who teaches his disciples in the ways of the good. Not via a master-and-slave relationship as it says, but through the time-honored master-and-student relationship in which the master mentors his student each step of the way.

מָה מום אָשִׁיב לַיהוָֹ\אדניאהדונהי כָּל ילי תַּגְמוּלוֹהִי עָלָי: כּוֹס

יְשׁוּעוֹת אֶשָּׂא וּבְשֵׁם יְהוָֹ\אדניאהדונהי אֶקְרָא: נְדָרַי

לַיהוָֹ\אדניאהדונהי אֲשַׁלֵּם נֶגְדָה נָא לְכָל עַמּוֹ: יָקָר בְּעֵינֵי

יְהוָֹ\אדניאהדונהי הַמָּוְתָה לַחֲסִידָיו:

*How can I repay Hashem for all that He had bestowed upon me? I raise a cup of salvation and call out in the Name of Hashem. I shall pay my vows to Hashem before all His people. It is difficult in the Eyes of Hashem, the death of His pious ones.*

אָנָּה יְהוָֹ‏‎אהדי‏אהדונהי‏ כִּי אֲנִי אֲנִי פי‏ עַבְדֶּךָ אני‏ עַבְדְּךָ פי‏ בֶּן
אֲמָתֶךָ פִּתַּחְתָּ לְמוֹסֵרָי: לְךָ אֶזְבַּח זֶבַח תּוֹדָה וּבְשֵׁם
יְהוָֹ‏‎אהדי‏אהדונהי‏ אֶקְרָא: נְדָרַי לַיהוָֹ‏‎אהדי‏אהדונהי‏ אֲשַׁלֵּם נֶגְדָה נָא
לְכָל עַמּוֹ: בְּחַצְרוֹת בֵּית ב״פ ראה‏ יְהוָֹ‏‎אהדי‏אהדונהי‏ בְּתוֹכֵכִי
יְרוּשָׁלִָם הַלְלוּיָהּ מום‏:

*Please, Hashem, I am Your servant. I am Your servant, then a son of Your handmaid. You have untied my bonds. To You I shall sacrifice a thanksgiving-offering and call out in the Name of Hashem. I shall pay my vows to Hashem before all His People, in the Courtyards of Hashem, within Jerusalem, Praise God. (Psalms 116:12-end)*

## MALCHUT - HAL'ELU

*All the nations of the world should praise God.* All the nations of the world require their own connection to God. It is not just the Israelites who have this privilege.

All nations must live by one universal rule: *Love thy neighbor as thyself.* Everyone must treat their fellow man with human dignity, sensitivity, and compassion. Prayer wasn't given to just the Israelites; the Torah and Kabbalah weren't given to just the Israelites. There are spiritual rites and rituals that Israelites perform, and there are spiritual connections that non-Israelites carry out. In Judaism, there are connections that men can perform, and there are connections that are exclusive to women. Each religion, according to Kabbalah, has its own path to the Light. But the one connection that applies to all nations of the world is *"Love thy neighbor."* Whether one is Catholic, Muslim, Jew, or Buddhist, we must all treat people with dignity. The only reason there is war between nations and chaos in society is because of the lack of compassion and sensitivity between people.

הַלְלוּ אֶת יְהוָֹ‏‎אהדי‏אהדונהי‏ כָּל יל‏ גּוֹיִם שַׁבְּחוּהוּ כָּל יל‏ הָאֻמִּים:
כִּי גָבַר עָלֵינוּ חַסְדּוֹ וֶאֱמֶת יְהוָֹ‏‎אהדי‏אהדונהי‏ לְעוֹלָם הַלְלוּיָהּ מום‏:

*Praise Hashem, all nations. Exalt Him, all peoples. For His kindness has overwhelmed us and the truth of Hashem is eternal, Praise God. (Psalms 117)*

## MALCHUT - HODU

The next four lines connect to four spiritual worlds. Spiritually speaking, some people in our world connect to the highest worlds while others connect to the middle and lower realms. The only way for humanity to achieve true unity is for each of us to let go of our ego and accept the fact that no one is higher or lower. It is only the ego that creates this distinction. If we consider ourselves on the same level as all of our fellow man, God responds and his energy reaches us on our own level. This is how we achieve oneness among men and God.

The Talmud reinforces this concept. We learn that a mosquito is actually on a much higher spiritual level than a man who isn't pursuing his spiritual work. A mosquito comes into this world to bite. As we all know, the mosquito does his job quite effectively. We came here to achieve a spiritual transformation. If the CEO of a major corporation and a factory worker are both doing their spiritual work, they are fulfilling their mission in life and are therefore on the same level in the eyes of God.[57]

These four verses connect to four different combinations of the *Yud Hei Vav Hei*. Each of these different combinations of letters is like different stages of transformers channeling currents of spiritual energy from various levels of the ten Sfirot to our physical realm.

1. "Yud יוד,     hy הי,     vyv ויו,     hy הי"     : the level of   Chochmah

2. "Yud יוד,     hy הי,     vav ואו,     jhy הי"     : the level of   Binah.

3. "Yud יוד,     ha הא,     vav ואו,     ha הא"     : the level of   Zeir Anpin[58]

4. "Yud יוד,     hh הה,     vv וו,     hh הה"     : the level of   Malchut

הוֹדוּ אהיה לַיהֹוָ֒הֿאהדיןֿואהדונֿהי כִּי    יוד הי ויו הי
אלף הי יוד הי

טוֹב והו אום כִּי לְעוֹלָם וַֿחַסְדּוֹ:

יֹאמַר נָא יִשְׂרָאֵל כִּי לְעוֹלָם    יוד הי ויו הי
אלף הי יוד הי

וַֿחַסְדּוֹ:

יֹאמְרוּ נָא בית ב"פ ראה אַהֲרֹן    יוד הא ואו הא
אלף הא יוד הא

כִּי לְעוֹלָם וַֿחַסְדּוֹ:

יֹאמְרוּ נָא יִרְאֵי יְֿהֹוָ֒האהדיןֿואהדונֿהי    יוד הה וו הה
אלף הה יוד הה

כִּי לְעוֹלָם וַֿחַסְדּוֹ:

*Give thanks to Hashem, for He is good, for His kindness is forever. Let Israel say so now, for His kindness is forever. Let the House of Aharon say so now, for His kindness is forever. Let those who fear Hashem say so now, for His kindness is forever.*

## MIN HAMITZAR

*From the straits I called upon God.* Unfortunately, most of us call upon God when we are in dire straits. We plead with God to fill our void, to loosen the collar around our necks.

---

57. Some people are content in the current positions in life because it fills their egos. These people need to work harder to pierce the veil of illusion that is stagnating their spiritual mission in life. Other people are never happy with where they are. Part of their work is to truly appreciate that they are doing their spiritual work. They should realize that they're on the same spiritual level as the people they envy as well as the people they consider to be on a lower level than themselves.

58. Zeir Anpin is a compacted dimension that enfolds the six dimensions of Chesed, Gvurah, Tiferet, Netzach, Hod, and Yesod as a unified whole.

To help us get a little breathing room, God will answer us during these trying times, provided we also call upon Him during good times and recognize His hand and influence in all of our good fortune.

The Zohar also teaches us that if we create a spiritual opening within ourselves no wider than the eye of a needle, God will answer us and show us the supernal gates. Why does the Zohar use the metaphor of the eye of a needle when it could have just said "make a tiny opening"? The eye of a needle might be microscopic, but it is a complete and pure opening. Our opening for spirituality could be a small and tiny, but there can be no doubt or uncertainty. It must be a complete opening.

מִן הַמֵּצַר קָרָאתִי יָהּ הּהּהּ עָנָנִי בַמֶּרְחָב יָהּ הּהּהּ: יְהֹוָ֨הַדנּ־יּאהדנּהּי יָהּ הּהּהּ:

לִי לֹא אִירָא מַה יַּעֲשֶׂה לִי אָדָם: יְהֹוָ֨הַדנּ־יּאהדנּהּי לִי בְּעֹזְרָי

וַאֲנִי אּ֑נּ אֶרְאֶה רּאהּ בְּשֹׂנְאָי: טוֹב וּהּ לַחֲסוֹת בַּיהֹוָ֨הַדנּ־יּאהדנּהּי

מִבְּטֹחַ בָּאָדָם: טוֹב וּהּ לַחֲסוֹת בַּיהֹוָ֨הַדנּ־יּאהדנּהּי מִבְּטֹחַ

בִּנְדִיבִים: כָּל יּלּ גּוֹיִם סְבָבוּנִי בְּשֵׁם יְהֹוָ֨הַדנּ־יּאהדנּהּי כִּי

אֲמִילַם: סַבּוּנִי גַם סְבָבוּנִי בְּשֵׁם יְהֹוָ֨הַדנּ־יּאהדנּהּי כִּי אֲמִילַם:

סַבּוּנִי כִדְבוֹרִים דֹּעֲכוּ כְּאֵשׁ קוֹצִים בְּשֵׁם יְהֹוָ֨הַדנּ־יּאהדנּהּי כִּי

אֲמִילַם: דָּחֹה דְחִיתַנִי לִנְפֹּל וַיהֹוָ֨הַדנּ־יּאהדנּהּי עֲזָרָנִי: עָזִּי מּוּם

וְזִמְרָת יָהּ הּהּהּ וַיְהִי לִי לִישׁוּעָה: קוֹל רִנָּה וִישׁוּעָה בְּאָהֳלֵי

צַדִּיקִים יְמִין יְהֹוָ֨הַדנּ־יּאהדנּהּי עֹשָׂה חָיִל וּמּבּ: יְמִין יְהֹוָ֨הַדנּ־יּאהדנּהּי

רוֹמֵמָה יְמִין יְהֹוָ֨הַדנּ־יּאהדנּהּי עֹשָׂה חָיִל וּמּבּ: לֹא אָמוּת כִּי אֶחְיֶה

וַאֲסַפֵּר מַעֲשֵׂי יָהּ הּהּהּ:

*Greatly from my distress I called out to God. Patient God answered me in His expansiveness. Hashem is with me, I shall not fear those who bear iniquities. What can man do to me? And sins, Hashem shall come to my rescue and cleanses.And I shall look upon my enemiesIt is good to take refuge in Hashem rather than to trust in man. It is better to take refuge in Hashem than to trust in noblemen. All the nations surrounded me. In the Name of Hashem, I shall cut them down. They surrounded me again and again. In the Name of Hashem, I shall cut them down. They surrounded me like bees, but are extinguished like a fire on thorns. With the Name of Hashem, I shall cut them down. They pushed me time and again to fall and Hashem came to my aid. The strength and cutting power of God were for me a salvation. The sound of song and salvation is in the tents of the righteous. The Right of Hashem does mighty things. The Right of Hashem is raised. The Right of Hashem does mighty things. I shall not die, But rather I shall live and tell of the deeds of God.*

יַסֹּר יִסְּרַנִּי יָהּ ההה וְלַמָּוֶת לֹא נְתָנָנִי: פִּתְחוּ לִי שַׁעֲרֵי צֶדֶק

אָבֹא בָם אוֹדֶה יָהּ ההה: זֶה הַשַּׁעַר לַיהֹוָאהדונהי צַדִּיקִים

יָבֹאוּ בוֹ:

*God has chastised me again and again, but He has not surrendered me to death. Open for me the gates of righteousness. I will go through them and give thanks to God. This is the Gate of Hashem, the righteous may go through it.*

## ODECHA

We have four verses that connect us to the four letters in *Yud Hei Vav Hei,* each verse is recited twice.[59]

י    אוֹדְךָ כִּי עֲנִיתָנִי וַתְּהִי לִי לִישׁוּעָה:

ה    אֶבֶן מָאֲסוּ הַבּוֹנִים הָיְתָה לְרֹאשׁ פִּנָּה:

ו    מֵאֵת יְהֹוָאהדונהי הָיְתָה זֹּאת הִיא נִפְלָאת בְּעֵינֵינוּ:

ה    זֶה הַיּוֹם גה.ן עָשָׂה יְהֹוָאהדונהי נָגִילָה וְנִשְׂמְחָה בוֹ:

*I am grateful to You, for You have answered me and have become my salvation. The stone that was rejected by the builders has become the main cornerstone. This came about from Hashem, it is wondrous in our eyes. Hashem has made this day, let us be glad and rejoice in it.*

## ANA

These four verses offer us a different pathway to Light. The numeric equivalent of *Yud Hei Vav Hei* is 52, which is also the numeric value of our physical realm of Malchut. Like the moon, Malchut has no Light of its own. These four verses help us, the Malchut, receive Light along the following circuits:

1.  The first verse is Malchut receiving from Chochmah.
2.  The second verse is Malchut receiving from Binah.
3.  The third verse is Malchut receiving from Zeir Anpin.
4.  The fourth verse is Malchut receiving from Chochmah, Binah, and Zeir Anpin collectively.

---

59. The Tetragrammaton is a powerful combination of Hebrew letters that literally transmits the spiritual forces of the Upper World into our physical existence. The four letters of the Tetragrammaton are יהוה.

אָנָּא לכב יְהֹוָ֨ה‏אדניאהדונהי הוֹשִׁיעָה נָּא:

אָנָּא לכב יְהֹוָ֨ה‏אדניאהדונהי הוֹשִׁיעָה נָּא:

אָנָּא לכב יְהֹוָ֨ה‏אדניאהדונהי הַצְלִיחָה נָּא:

אָנָּא לכב יְהֹוָ֨ה‏אדניאהדונהי הַצְלִיחָה נָּא:

*We beseech You, Hashem, save us now. We beseech You, Hashem, save us now. We beseech You, Hashem, give us success now. We beseech You, Hashem, give us success now.*

## BARUCH HABA

These next four verses are the regular connections to the *Yud Hei Vav Hei* Each verse is recited twice.

בָּרוּךְ הַבָּא בְּשֵׁם יְהֹוָ֨ה‏אדניאהדונהי בֵּרַכְנוּכֶם מִבֵּית ב"פ ראה

יְהֹוָ֨ה‏אדניאהדונהי:

אֵל יְהֹוָ֨ה‏אדניאהדונהי וַיָּאֶר לָנוּ מום אִסְרוּ חַג בַּעֲבֹתִים עַד

קַרְנוֹת הַמִּזְבֵּחַ נג"ד:

אֵלִי אַתָּה וְאוֹדֶךָּ אֱלֹהַי דמב אֲרוֹמְמֶךָּ:

הוֹדוּ אהיה לַיהֹוָ֨ה‏אדניאהדונהי כִּי טוֹב והו כִּי לְעוֹלָם חַסְדּוֹ:

*Blessed is the one who comes in the Name of Hashem. We bless you from The House of Hashem. Hashem is God, He illuminates for us. Tie the holiday-offering with ropes until the corners of the Altar. You are my God and I thank You, my God, and I shall exalt You. Be grateful to Hashem for He is good. For His kindness is forever. (Psalms 118)*

## HODU

This section contains 26 verses, which happens to be the same numerical value as the Tetragrammaton.[59] Each one of these verses also correlates to 26 different angels. We do not know the specific cosmic function and role of most of these angels. They are, however, connected to the Tetragrammaton via these 26 verses. In turn, the Tetragrammaton is our connection to the Upper World directly above us, a realm known as Zeir Anpin.[60] We also know that Zeir Anpin and the angels who reside there are responsible for all the fulfillment, miracles, pleasure, sustenance, and happiness that we can achieve in this

---

61. Humanity is likened to the moon, for we both have no light of our own. The light of the moon is derived from the sun. The spiritual Light of man is derived from the Upper Word realm of Zeir Anpin.

physical world. We can capture all these qualities in one step through these 26 verses, the Tetragrammaton, and the 26 angels.

When we recite this section, we should meditate to fulfill all the lacks in our life – the lacks that we are aware of, as well as any lacks that we're not yet cognizant of.

י׳

אדריאל

וְהוּ אוֹם **הוֹדוּ** אהיה **לַיהֹוָה**אהדיאיאהדינהי **כִּי טוֹב**

כִּי לְעוֹלָם וַחַסְדּוֹ ג׳ הויות: זְיְוָד

*Give thanks to Hashem for He is good, for His kindness endures forever.*

ברכיאל

יכה **הוֹדוּ** אהיה **לֵאלֹהֵי** דמב **הָאֱלֹהִים**

כִּי לְעוֹלָם וַחַסְדּוֹ ג׳ הויות: זְיְוָד

*Give thanks to the God of all the heavenly powers, for His kindness endures forever.*

גועיאל

**הוֹדוּ** אהיה **לַאֲדֹנֵי הָאֲדֹנִים**

כִּי לְעוֹלָם וַחַסְדּוֹ ג׳ הויות: זְיְוָד

*Give thanks to the Master of all masters, for His kindness endures forever.*

דורעיאל

מ״ב **לְעֹשֵׂה נִפְלָאוֹת גְּדֹלוֹת לְבַדּוֹ**

כִּי לְעוֹלָם וַחַסְדּוֹ ג׳ הויות: זְיְוָד

*To the One Who alone performs great wonders, for His kindness endures forever.*

הדריאל

**לְעֹשֵׂה הַשָּׁמַיִם** י״פ טל **בִּתְבוּנָה**

כִּי לְעוֹלָם וַחַסְדּוֹ ג׳ הויות: זְיְוָד

*To the One Who made the Heavens with understanding, For His kindness endures forever.*

ויעדיאל

**לְרֹקַע הָאָרֶץ עַל הַמָּיִם**

כִּי לְעוֹלָם וַחַסְדּוֹ ג׳ הויות: זְיְוָד

*To the One Who spreads out the earth upon the waters, for His kindness endures forever.*

וברזיאל

לְעֹשֵׂה אוֹרִים ה ּ גְּדֹלִים

כִּי לְעוֹלָם וַחֲסְדּוֹ גֹּ׳ הַיּוּת: יְוָד

*To the One Who made great Lights, for His kindness endures forever.*

וזניאל

אֶת הַשֶּׁמֶשׁ לְמֶמְשֶׁלֶת בַּיּוֹם גגד, ֹח

כִּי לְעוֹלָם וַחֲסְדּוֹ גֹּ׳ הַיּוּת: יְוָד

*The sun for the reign of the day, for His kindness endures forever.*

טהוריאל

אֶת הַיָּרֵחַ וְכוֹכָבִים לְמֶמְשָׁלוֹת בַּלַּיְלָה מלה

כִּי לְעוֹלָם וַחֲסְדּוֹ גֹּ׳ הַיּוּת: יְוָד

*The moon and the stars for the reign of the night, for His kindness endures forever.*

ידידיאל

לְמַכֵּה מִצְרַיִם מצ בִּבְכוֹרֵיהֶם

כִּי לְעוֹלָם וַחֲסְדּוֹ גֹּ׳ הַיּוּת: יְוָד

*To the One Who smote Egypt through their firstborn, for His kindness endures forever.*

ה

כרוביאל

וַיּוֹצֵא יִשְׂרָאֵל מִתּוֹכָם

כִּי לְעוֹלָם וַחֲסְדּוֹ גֹּ׳ הַיּוּת: הָי

*And Who took Israel out of their midst, for His kindness endures forever.*

להטיאל

בְּיָד וְחֲזָקָה וּבִזְרוֹעַ נְטוּיָה

כִּי לְעוֹלָם וַחֲסְדּוֹ גֹּ׳ הַיּוּת: הָי

*With a strong Hand and with an outstretched Arm, for His kindness endures forever.*

מהגביאל

לְגֹזֵר יַם ־יּ סוּף לִגְזָרִים

כִּי לְעוֹלָם חַסְדּוֹ ־ג׳ הִוּוּת: הָיְ

*To the One Who divided the Sea of Reeds into parts, for His kindness endures forever.*

נוריאל

וְהֶעֱבִיר יִשְׂרָאֵל בְּתוֹכוֹ

כִּי לְעוֹלָם חַסְדּוֹ ־ג׳ הִוּוּת: הָיְ

*And Who caused Israel to pass through It, for His kindness endures forever.*

נתצניאל

וְנִעֵר פַּרְעֹה וְחֵילוֹ בְיַם ־יּ סוּף

כִּי לְעוֹלָם חַסְדּוֹ ־ג׳ הִוּוּת: הָיְ

*And threw Pharo and his army into the Sea of Reeds, for His kindness endures forever.*

ו

נוריאל

לְמוֹלִיךְ עַמּוֹ בַּמִּדְבָּר

כִּי לְעוֹלָם חַסְדּוֹ ־ג׳ הִוּוּת: וָיְוַ

*To the One Who led His Nation, Israel, through the wilderness, for His kindness endures forever.*

סרעיאל

לְמַכֵּה מְלָכִים גְּדֹלִים

כִּי לְעוֹלָם חַסְדּוֹ ־ג׳ הִוּוּת: וָיְוַ

*To the One Who smote kings, for His kindness endures forever.*

עעיאל

וַיַּהֲרֹג מְלָכִים אַדִּירִים ־הּ־ִי

כִּי לְעוֹלָם חַסְדּוֹ ־ג׳ הִוּוּת: וָיְוַ

*And slew mighty kings, for His kindness endures forever.*

פקדיאל

## לְסִיחוֹן מֶלֶךְ הָאֱמֹרִי

כִּי לְעוֹלָם חַסְדּוֹ: ג' הַוָּיוֹת: וָיֶו

*Sichon, the king of the Emorites, for His kindness endures forever.*

צרופיאל

## וּלְעוֹג מֶלֶךְ הַבָּשָׁן

כִּי לְעוֹלָם חַסְדּוֹ: ג' הַוָּיוֹת: וָיֶו

*And Og, the king of Bashan, for His kindness endures forever.*

קדושיאל

## וְנָתַן אַרְצָם לְנַחֲלָה

כִּי לְעוֹלָם חַסְדּוֹ: ג' הַוָּיוֹת: וָיֶו

*And presented their land as a heritage, for His kindness endures forever.*

## ה

רוממיאל

## נַחֲלָה לְיִשְׂרָאֵל עַבְדּוֹ

כִּי לְעוֹלָם חַסְדּוֹ: ג' הַוָּיוֹת: הֵא

*A heritage for Israel, His servant, for His kindness endures forever.*

שומריאל

## שֶׁבְּשִׁפְלֵנוּ זָכַר לָנוּ מום

כִּי לְעוֹלָם חַסְדּוֹ: ג' הַוָּיוֹת: הֵא

*In our lowliness He remembered us, for His kindness endures forever.*

שומריאל

## וַיִּפְרְקֵנוּ מִצָּרֵינוּ

כִּי לְעוֹלָם חַסְדּוֹ: ג' הַוָּיוֹת: הֵא

*And released us from our tormentors, for His kindness endures forever.*

תומכיאל

נֹתֵן לֶחֶם ג הויות לְכָל יה ארני בָּשָׂר

כִּי לְעוֹלָם וַסְדוֹ ג הויות: הָי

*He gives nourishment to all flesh, for His kindness endures forever.*

תהפיאל

הוֹדוּ אהיה לְאֵל הַשָּׁמַיִם יפ טל

כִּי לְעוֹלָם וַסְדוֹ ג הויות: הָי

*Give thanks to the God of the Heavens, for His kindness endures forever. (Psalms 136)*

## NISHMAT

This section is recited on all holidays and Shabbat. It is our connection, our vessel, to capture the additional spiritual energy that is made available on holidays and Shabbat. We always recite these verses in the morning – except for on Pesach, where we recite it at night.

Rabbi Avraham Azulai teaches us that when nightfall arrives, a part of our soul leaves us for the Upper Worlds, even when we're awake, which is why we feel tired as the evening grows on. At midnight, the soul returns. Before we go to bed, there is a special connection we make, known as the *Shema*, which acts like a safety chord between our body and soul. This chord remains attached to our body as our soul ascends into the Upper Worlds. At midnight, the chord "reels" the soul back into the body. The *Shema* also protects the body while the soul has vacated.

On Pesach, this entire process does not occur. Our soul does not need recharging on the night of Pesach because the holiday itself provides us with that charge. Further, we do not have to recite the *Shema* since our soul remains with us. We do not require any extra protection on Pesach night.

This connection of *Nishmat* provides us with additional protection on all other nights, for the remainder of the year, each night our soul leaves us.

נִשְׁמַת כָּל יל וזי בינה עה תְּבָרֵךְ אֶת שִׁמְךָ יְהֹוָאהדונהי

אֱלֹהֵינוּ ילה וְרוּחַ כָּל יל בָּשָׂר תְּפָאֵר וּתְרוֹמֵם זִכְרְךָ מַלְכֵּנוּ

תָּמִיד עה נתה. מִן הָעוֹלָם וְעַד הָעוֹלָם אַתָּה אֵל. וּמִבַּלְעָדֶיךָ

אֵין לָנוּ מום מֶלֶךְ גּוֹאֵל וּמוֹשִׁיעַ. פּוֹדֶה וּמַצִּיל. וְעוֹנֶה וּמְרַחֵם

אברהם בְּכָל לכב עֵת צָרָה וְצוּקָה.

*The soul of every living thing shall bless Your Name, Hashem, our God; and the spirit of all flesh shall always glorify and exalt Your remembrance, our King. From (this) world to the world (to come), You are God. And other than You, we have no redeeming or saving king. Liberator, rescuer, sustainer, and merciful. At any time of distress and anguish.*

אֵין לָנוּ מֶלֶךְ עוֹזֵר וְסוֹמֵךְ כּוּק אֶלָּא אָתָּה: אֱלֹהֵי דמב
הָרִאשׁוֹנִים וְהָאַחֲרוֹנִים. אֱלֽוֹהַּ מ״ב כָּל יל׳ בְּרִיּוֹת. אֲדוֹן אני
כָּל יל׳ תּוֹלָדוֹת. הַמְהֻלָּל בְּכָל לכב הַתִּשְׁבָּחוֹת. הַמְנַהֵג
עוֹלָמוֹ בְּחֶסֶד ע״ב וּבְרִיּוֹתָיו בְּרַחֲמִים מצפצ׳. וַיהֹוָֽהָאדני ו׃הׂ
אֱלֹהִים יל׳ אֱמֶת אהיה פ׳ אהיה לֹא יָנוּם וְלֹא יִישָׁן. הַמְּעוֹרֵר
יְשֵׁנִים וְהַמֵּקִיץ נִרְדָּמִים. מְחַיֶּה ס״ג מֵתִים. וְרוֹפֵא חוֹלִים מ״ה
יהוה. פּוֹקֵחַ עִוְרִים. וְזוֹקֵף כְּפוּפִים. הַמֵּשִׂיחַ אִלְּמִים.
וְהַמַּפְעָנֵחַ נֶעְלָמִים. וּלְךָ לְבַדְּךָ אֲנַחְנוּ מוֹדִים מאה׃וְאִלּוּ פִינוּ
מָלֵא שִׁירָה כַּיָּם יל׳. וּלְשׁוֹנֵנוּ רִנָּה כַּהֲמוֹן גַּלָּיו. וְשִׂפְתוֹתֵינוּ
שֶׁבַח כְּמֶרְחֲבֵי רָקִיעַ. וְעֵינֵינוּ מְאִירוֹת כַּשֶּׁמֶשׁ וְכַיָּרֵחַ.
וְיָדֵינוּ פְרוּשׂוֹת כְּנִשְׁרֵי שָׁמָיִם י״ב טל׳. וְרַגְלֵינוּ קַלּוֹת כָּאַיָּלוֹת.
אֵין אֲנַחְנוּ מַסְפִּיקִין לְהוֹדוֹת לְךָ יְהֹוָֽהָאדני ו׃הׂ אֱלֹהֵינוּ יל׳.
וּלְבָרֵךְ אֶת שִׁמְךָ מַלְכֵּנוּ. עַל אַחַת מֵאֶלֶף אַלְפֵי אֲלָפִים
וְרוֹב רִבֵּי רְבָבוֹת פְּעָמִים. הַטּוֹבוֹת נִסִּים וְנִפְלָאוֹת
שֶׁעָשִׂיתָ עִמָּנוּ וְעִם אֲבוֹתֵינוּ.

*We have no helping or supporting king other than You. God of the first and of the last, God of all creatures, Master of all generations, Which is extolled through a multitude of praises, Which guides Its world with kindness and Its creatures with mercy. Hashem is a God of truth. It is awake, neither slumbers nor sleeps. It rouses the sleepers and awakens the slumberers, resuscitates the dead, heals the sick, gives sight to the blind, straightens the bent, makes the mute speak, deciphers the unknown — and to You alone we give thanks. Were our mouth full of songs as the sea, and our tongue as full of joyous song as its multitude of waves, and our lips as full of praise as the breadth of the sky, and our eyes as brilliant as the sun and the moon, and our hands as outspread as eagles of the sky, and our feet as swift as hinds. we still could not thank You sufficiently, Hashem, our God, and bless Your Name, Our King, for even one of the thousand, thousands of thousands, and myriad of times (that You have granted us) favors, miracles, and wonders that You performed for us and for our forefathers.*

מִלְּפָנִים מִמִּצְרַיִם מצר וּגְאַלְתָּנוּ יְהֹוָהאהדונהי אֱלֹהֵינוּ ילה.

מִבֵּית ב״פ ראה עֲבָדִים פְּדִיתָנוּ. בְּרָעָב זַנְתָּנוּ. וּבְשָׂבָע

כִּלְכַּלְתָּנוּ. מֵחֶרֶב הִצַּלְתָּנוּ. מִדֶּבֶר מִלַּטְתָּנוּ. וּמֵחֳלָאִים

רָעִים וְרַבִּים דִּלִּיתָנוּ: עַד הֵנָּה עֲזָרוּנוּ רַחֲמֶיךָ וְלֹא עֲזָבוּנוּ

וַחֲסָדֶיךָ. עַל כֵּן אֵבָרִים שֶׁפִּלַּגְתָּ בָּנוּ. וְרוּחַ וּנְשָׁמָה שֶׁנָּפַחְתָּ

בְּאַפֵּינוּ. וְלָשׁוֹן אֲשֶׁר שַׂמְתָּ בְּפִינוּ. הֵן הֵם, יוֹדוּ וִיבָרְכוּ.

וִישַׁבְּחוּ. וִיפָאֲרוּ. אֶת שִׁמְךָ מַלְכֵּנוּ תָּמִיד עה גתה. כִּי כָל ילי

פֶּה עה מום לְךָ יוֹדֶה. וְכָל לָשׁוֹן לְךָ תִשָּׁבַע. וְכָל עַיִן מ״ה בריבוע

לְךָ תְצַפֶּה. וְכָל בֶּרֶךְ לְךָ תִכְרַע. וְכָל קוֹמָה לְפָנֶיךָ סמ״ב

תִשְׁתַּחֲוֶה. וְהַלְּבָבוֹת יִירָאוּךָ וְהַקֶּרֶב וְהַכְּלָיוֹת יְזַמְּרוּ

לִשְׁמְךָ. כַּדָּבָר ראה שֶׁנֶּאֱמַר כָּל ילי עַצְמוֹתַי תֹּאמַרְנָה

יְהֹוָהאהדונהי מִי ילי כָמוֹךָ מַצִּיל עָנִי מֵחָזָק פהל מִמֶּנּוּ וְעָנִי

וְאֶבְיוֹן מִגֹּזְלוֹ: שַׁוְעַת עֲנִיִּים אַתָּה תִשְׁמַע. צַעֲקַת הַדַּל

תַּקְשִׁיב וְתוֹשִׁיעַ: וְכָתוּב רַנְּנוּ צַדִּיקִים בַּיהֹוָהאהדונהי

לַיְשָׁרִים נָאוָה תְהִלָּה:

*At first You redeemed us from Egypt, Hashem, our God, and liberated us from the house of bondage. In famine You nourished us, and in plenty You sustained us. From the sword You saved us; from plague You let us escape; and from severe and numerous diseases You spared us. Until now Your mercy has helped us, and Your kindness has not forsaken us. Therefore, the organs that You differentiated within us, spirit and soul that You breathed into our nostrils, and the tongue that You placed in our mouth, all of them shall thank and bless, praise and glorify Your Name, our King, continuously. For every mouth shall thank You, every tongue shall praise You, every eye shall look forward to You, every knee shall bend to You, every erect spine shall prostrate itself before You; the hearts shall fear You, the guts and kidneys shall sing (praises) to Your Name, as it is written: "All my bones shall say: 'Hashem, who is like You?' You save the poor man from one stronger than him; the poor and destitute from one who would rob him." The outcry of the poor You hear. The screams of the destitute You listen to and save them. As it is written: Sing, righteous of Hashem, the straight are praiseworthy.*

### YITZCHAK AND RIVKAH

Yitzchak, son of the patriarch Abraham, successfully prayed for his wife Rivkah to have a baby. Kabbalah teaches us the lesson of this story. All of us, especially at this juncture, must pray for others who are in need of financial, health, personal, or emotional sustenance. The only way our own prayers will be answered is for us to pray for others with a genuine heart.

בְּפִי יְשָׁרִים תִּתְרוֹמָם:

*By the mouths of the upright, You shall be exalted.*

וּבְשִׂפְתֵי צַדִּיקִים תִּתְבָּרַךְ:

*And by the lips of the righteous, You shall be blessed.*

וּבִלְשׁוֹן וְ חֲסִידִים תִּתְקַדָּשׁ:

*And by the tongues of the pious, You shall be sanctified.*

וּבְקֶרֶב קְדוֹשִׁים תִּתְהַלָּל:

*And among the holy ones, You shall be lauded.*

### BMIK'HLOT

This prayer refers to our world of Malchut – not just to its physical aspect, but to its true spiritual essence. This connection to the spiritual quality of Malchut signifies the concept of mind over matter.[61]

בְּמִקְהֲלוֹת רִבְבוֹת עַמְּךָ בֵּית יִשְׂרָאֵל. שֶׁכֵּן וְחוֹבַת

כָּל הַיְצוּרִים לְפָנֶיךָ

*In the assemblies of the myriads of Your people, the house of Israel. For the duty of all creatures perform before You,*

---

62. Contrary to popular belief, the physical world is not a hindrance or blockage preventing us from connecting to the Creator. Instead, physical matter is our vehicle to make our connection. We accomplish this through the power of mind over matter. Each time we achieve mind over matter, we make the highest possible connection to the Creator. Not reacting to external events is a lower level of mind over matter that generates Light in our daily lives. The purpose of not reacting to external events, however, is to eventually generate enough Light that we eventually reach a spiritual level where we can attain *total* mind over matter. For example, if we can attain a consciousness of not reacting to, say, a car accident, nothing will happen. We would escape physical injury by transcending the physical world. Physical matter was created not so that we could use it or be limited by it, but so that we could learn how to attain mastery over it. Once we achieve this kind of nonreactive state of mind, nothing physical will influence our life, giving way to the concept of immortality.

יְהֹוָהאהדינהי אֱלֹהֵינוּ ילה וֵאלֹהֵי ילה אֲבוֹתֵינוּ לכב לְהוֹדוֹת. לְהַלֵּל

ללה. לְשַׁבֵּחַ. לְפָאֵר. לְרוֹמֵם. לְהַדֵּר. וּלְנַצֵּחַ. עַל כָּל ילה

דִּבְרֵי ראה שִׁירוֹת וְתִשְׁבָּחוֹת דָּוִד בֶּן יִשַׁי עַבְדְּךָ פִּי מְשִׁיחֶךָ:

*Hashem, our God and the God of our forefathers, is to thank, laud, praise, glorify, exalt, adore, and conduct all expressions of the songs and praises of David, the son of Yishai, Your servant, Your anointed.*

## YISHTABACH

The first word of this connection has the numerical value of 72, linking us to the 72 Names of God.[62] The next word has the numerical value of 720 – ten times the power of the 72 Names.

Next, we receive the power of King Solomon through his Hebrew name, which is encoded inside this verse. King Solomon was known as Solomon the Wise because of his tremendous spiritual knowledge. We can capture his energy of wisdom by virtue of this connection. In the last section of this prayer, we also have letters spelling out Avraham's name. Kabbalistically, Avraham denotes the power of sharing. By combining the energy of Avraham (sharing) and King Solomon (wisdom), we learn how *not* to share foolishly but instead to share with wisdom.[63]

S    O    L    O    M    O    N

◄─────────────────────────

וּבְכֵן יִשְׁתַּבַּח שִׁמְךָ לָעַד מַלְכֵּנוּ הָאֵל לאה הַמֶּלֶךְ

הַגָּדוֹל להו וְהַקָּדוֹשׁ בַּשָּׁמַיִם וּבָאָרֶץ: כִּי לְךָ נָאֶה

יְהֹוָהאהדינהי אֱלֹהֵינוּ ילה וֵאלֹהֵי ילה אֲבוֹתֵינוּ לכב לְעוֹלָם וָעֶד:

(1 שִׁיר (2 וּשְׁבָחָה. (3 הַלֵּל (4 וְזִמְרָה. (5 עֹז (6 וּמֶמְשָׁלָה. (7 נֶצַח.

(8 גְּדֻלָּה. (9 גְבוּרָה ריו. (10 תְּהִלָּה.

*May Your Name be praised forever, our King, the God, the great and holy King, Who is in the Heavens and in the earth. For to You are befitting, Hashem our God and the God of our fathers, forever and ever: 1) song 2) and praise 3) exultation 4) and melody 5) power 6) and dominion 7) eternity 8) greatness 9) valor 10) praise*

---

63. The 72 Names of God is a formula Moses used to engineer the miracles in Egypt. This formula was concealed inside the holy Zohar for more than 2,000 years. It consists of 72 three-letter sequences encoded inside the story of Exodus in the Torah. Each three-letter sequence gives us a particular power to overcome the numerous negative traits of human nature, in the same way that Moses used this spiritual technology to overpower the laws of mother nature.

64. Many people share to gratify their own ego. Some people share too much and are depleted. Others do not share enough and therefore disconnect themselves from the Light. We must learn how to strike that elusive balance between sharing and receiving.

11) וְתִפְאָרֶת. 12) קְדֻשָׁה. 13) וּמַלְכוּת. בְּרָכוֹת וְהוֹדָאוֹת

לְשִׁמְךָ הַגָּדוֹל לּהּ וְהַקָּדוֹשׁ. וּמֵעוֹלָם וְעַד עוֹלָם אַתָּה אֵל.

בָּרוּךְ אַתָּה יְהוֹ‑אדנּהּ‑אהדנּהּ מֶלֶךְ גָּדוֹל לּהּ וּמְהֻלָּל בַּתִּשְׁבָּחוֹת.

אֵל הַהוֹדָאוֹת.

*11) and glory 12) holiness 13) and sovereignty. Blessings and thanksgiving to Your great and holy Name from this world to the world to come. You are God. Blessed are You, Hashem, King, Who is great and lauded with praise. God of thanksgiving.*

אָדוֹן אני הַנִּפְלָאוֹת.    A

בּוֹרֵא כָּל ילי הַנְּשָׁמוֹת.    V

רִבּוֹן כָּל ילי    R

הַמַּעֲשִׂים. הַבּוֹחֵר בְּשִׁירֵי זִמְרָה.    H A

מֶלֶךְ אֵל חֵי הָעוֹלָמִים: אָמֵן:    M

*Master of the wonders. Creator of the souls. Master of all deeds. One Who chooses melodious songs of praise. The King, the God Who gives life to all the worlds, amen.*

### L'SHEM YIKHUD – PREPARING FOR THE FOURTH CUP OF WINE

L'Shem Yikhud prepares us for the intense amount of energy coming to us via the drinking of the wine.

לְשֵׁם יְחוּד קוּדְשָׁא בְּרִיךְ הוּא וּשְׁכִינְתֵּיהּ בִּדְחִילוּ וּרְחִימוּ

וּרְחִימוּ וּדְחִילוּ לְיַחֲדָא שֵׁם יוּד קֵי בְּוָאו קֵי בִּיחוּדָא

שְׁלִים יהוה בְּשֵׁם כָּל ילי יִשְׂרָאֵל,

*For the sake of unifying The Holy One, blessed be It, and Its Shechinah, with fear and mercy, and with mercy and fear, to unify the name of Yud Key with Vav Key completely, in the name of all Israel,*

הִנְנִי מוּכָן וּמְזוּמָן לְקַיֵּם מִצְוַת כּוֹס מוּם רְבִיעִי שֶׁל אַרְבַּע

כּוֹסוֹת, וִיהִי נֹעַם אֲדֹנָי אֱלֹהֵינוּ יה. עָלֵינוּ וּמַעֲשֵׂה יָדֵינוּ

כּוֹנְנָה עָלֵינוּ וּמַעֲשֵׂה יָדֵינוּ כּוֹנְנֵהוּ:

*I am ready and willing to apply the connection of Fourth Cup out of Four Cups, and may the pleasantness of Hashem, our God, be upon us, and establish the action of our hands upon us and establish the action of our hands.*

### THE FOURTH CUP OF WINE – ASIYAH

There are four cups of wine poured during the course of the Seder. These four cups signify and connect us to the four-letter name of God – the Tetragrammaton[59] – and four Upper Worlds in our spiritual atmosphere. The names of these worlds are Atzilut, Briah, Yetzirah, Asiyah.

בָּרוּךְ אַתָּה יְהוָֹהֵאהדונהי אֱלֹהֵינוּ יה. מֶלֶךְ הָעוֹלָם

בּוֹרֵא פְּרִי הַגָּפֶן:

*Blessed are You, Hashem, our God, King of the universe, Who creates the fruit of the vine.*

We drink while leaning to the left and then recite the last blessing.

### THE FINAL BLESSING

This blessing elevates the sparks of soul residing inside the wine. All the food and drink that arrives at our table on a holiday has a definite purpose. There is a spark of a soul residing within it that requires elevation into the Upper Worlds. By blessing the food and eating it, we elevate the spark. The food that we receive is never just by coincidence.[64]

בָּרוּךְ אַתָּה יְהוָֹהֵאהדונהי אֱלֹהֵינוּ יה. מֶלֶךְ הָעוֹלָם עַל הַגֶּפֶן

וְעַל פְּרִי הַגֶּפֶן וְעַל תְּנוּבַת הַשָּׂדֶה וְעַל אֶרֶץ חֶמְדָּה

טוֹבָה אכא וּרְחָבָה שֶׁרָצִיתָ וְהִנְחַלְתָּ לַאֲבוֹתֵינוּ לֶאֱכֹל מִפִּרְיָהּ

וְלִשְׂבּוֹעַ מִטּוּבָהּ.

*Blessed are You, Hashem, our God, King of the universe, for the vine and the fruit of the vine, and for the produce of the field. And for a desirable, good, and spacious land that You were pleased to give our forefathers as a heritage, to eat of its fruit and to be satisfied with its goodness.*

---

66. The Light has infinite power to compute each person's personal correction, based upon all his previous lifetimes and his particular connection to every speck of matter that he comes into contact with. Whether we are cognizant or not, everything in our life holds a deeper spiritual significance.

רַחֵם אברהם יְהֹוָאדְהֲיאהדונהי אֱלֹהֵינוּ ילה עָלֵינוּ וְעַל יִשְׂרָאֵל עַמֶּךָ

וְעַל יְרוּשָׁלַיִם עִירֶךָ וְעַל הַר צִיּוֹן יוסף מִשְׁכַּן כְּבוֹדֶךָ לכב.

וְעַל מִזְבָּחֶךָ. וְעַל הֵיכָלֶךָ. וּבְנֵה יְרוּשָׁלַיִם עִיר בֹזֹחֹזֹךְ, סנדלפון, ערי

הַקֹּדֶשׁ בִּמְהֵרָה בְיָמֵינוּ. וְהַעֲלֵנוּ לְתוֹכָהּ. וְשַׂמְּחֵנוּ בְּבִנְיָנָהּ.

וּנְבָרֶכְךָ עָלֶיהָ פהל בִּקְדֻשָּׁה וּבְטָהֳרָה.

*Have mercy, Hashem, our God, on us and on Israel, Your people; on Jerusalem, Your city; on the mount of Zion, the resting place of Your glory; Your altar and Your temple. Rebuild Jerusalem, the holy city, speedily, in our days. Bring us up into it, gladden us in its rebuilding, and we shall bless You upon it in holiness and purity.*

---

**On Shabbat**

וּרְצֵה וְהַחֲלִיצֵנוּ בְּיוֹם גנד, ח, הַשַּׁבָּת הַזֶּה והו.

*Favor us and strengthen us on this day of Shabbat,*

---

וְשַׂמְּחֵנוּ בְּיוֹם גנד, ח וְחַג הַמַּצּוֹת הַזֶּה והו. בְּיוֹם גנד, ח טוֹב והו

מִקְרָא קֹדֶשׁ הַזֶּה והו. כִּי אַתָּה טוֹב והו וּמֵטִיב לַכֹּל יה אדני.

וְנוֹדֶה לְּךָ יְהֹוָאדְהֲיאהדונהי אֱלֹהֵינוּ ילה עַל הָאָרֶץ וְעַל פְּרִי

הַגָּפֶן, בָּרוּךְ אַתָּה יְהֹוָאדְהֲיאהדונהי עַל הָאָרֶץ וְעַל פְּרִי הַגָּפֶן.

*And grant us happiness on the day of this feast of Matzot, on this holiday of holy reading. For You are good; You do good to all; and we thank You, Hashem, our God, for the land and for the fruit of the vine. Blessed are You, Hashem, for the land and for (its) fruit of the vine.*

### STAGE 15: NIRTZAH

# נִרְצָה

Through the actions of *Nirtzah*, we are ensuring that all our efforts and requests made thus far are accepted into the Upper World. We are using the power of certainty to guarantee that we have the power to get out of "Egypt" (chaos). We are injecting certainty into the process and into the outcome. We want everyone around the world who is taking part in the Pesach Seder to successfully complete their job as well.

Before we recite *Nirtzah*, we must remove any uncertainty or doubts from our consciousness.

וַחֲסַל סִדּוּר פֶּסַח כְּהִלְכָתוֹ כְּכָל מִשְׁפָּטוֹ וְחֻקָּתוֹ. כַּאֲשֶׁר זָכִינוּ לְסַדֵּר אוֹתוֹ. כֵּן נִזְכֶּה לַעֲשׂוֹתוֹ. זָךְ יּיי שׁוֹכֵן מְעוֹנָה. קוֹמֵם קְהַל עֲדַת מִי ילי מָנָה פּיי. בְּקָרוֹב נַהֵל נִטְעֵי כַנָּה. פְּדוּיִם לְצִיּוֹן יוֹסֵף בְּרִנָּה:

*The Seder is now concluded in accordance with its laws, with all its ordinances and statutes. Just as we were privileged to arrange it, so may we merit to perform it. O Pure One, Which dwells on high, raise up the countless congregation; soon guide the offshoots of Your plants, redeemed, to Zion with glad song.*

### L'SHANAH

We sing *next year in Jerusalem* because we can genuinely bring about the age of Messiah, immortality, the resurrection of the dead, and the Temple in Jerusalem if we just keep the consciousness of Pesach. A simple enough idea, but one that requires extraordinary spiritual strength and willpower.

The problem is further compounded by our short memory. We tend to forget the feeling and intensity of energy now being aroused as soon as we go back to the "real" world. It's tempting to succumb to the illusions of chaos and pressure that confront us in daily life. The moment we react to them, we allow the doubts to set in. Then it's game over. If we want to really see the dawning of a new day, we must believe in the freedom we have achieved tonight. We must have certainty when the first test appears. And, most important, each day of the year we must remember Pesach. A daily moment of remembrance will ensure permanent freedom from chaos.

לְשָׁנָה הַבָּאָה בִּירוּשָׁלָיִם הַבְּנוּיָה: ג"פ

*Next year in rebuilt Jerusalem*
(We repeat this three times.)

❧❧❧

To manifest all the power of Pesach we engage in song. These songs are structured according to the 22 letters of the Hebrew alphabet.

### UVCHEN

This connects us to the actual point at midnight when chaos was removed from the lives of the Israelites some 3,400 years ago.

וּבְכֵן ע"פ וַיְהִי בַּחֲצִי הַלַּיְלָה מלה:

*It came to pass at midnight.*

אָז רוֹב נִסִּים הִפְלֵאתָ בַּלַּיְלָה מלה. בְּרֹאשׁ אַשְׁמוּרֶת זֶה
הַלַּיְלָה מלה. גֵּר צֶדֶק נִצַּחְתּוֹ כְּנֶחֱלַק לוֹ לַיְלָה מלה.
וַיְהִי בַּחֲצִי הַלַּיְלָה מלה:

*You have, then, performed many wonders by night. At the head of the watchers of this night. To the righteous convert (Abraham) You gave triumph by dividing for him the night. It came to pass at midnight.*

דַּנְתָּ מֶלֶךְ גְּרָר בַּחֲלוֹם הַלַּיְלָה מלה. הִפְחַדְתָּ אֲרַמִּי בְּאֶמֶשׁ
לַיְלָה מלה. וַיִּשַׂר יִשְׂרָאֵל יָשַׂר לְאֵל וַיּוּכַל לוֹ לַיְלָה מלה.
וַיְהִי בַּחֲצִי הַלַּיְלָה מלה:

*You judged the king of Grar (Avimelech) in a dream by night. You frightened the Aramean (Lavan) in the dark of night. Israel (Jacob) fought with an angel and overcame him by night. It came to pass at midnight.*

זֶרַע בְּכוֹרֵי פַתְרוֹס מָחַצְתָּ בַּחֲצִי הַלַּיְלָה מלה. וְחֵילָם לֹא
מָצְאוּ בְּקוּמָם בַּלַּיְלָה מלה. טִיסַת נְגִיד חֲרֹשֶׁת סִלִּיתָ
בְּכוֹכְבֵי לַיְלָה מלה. וַיְהִי בַּחֲצִי הַלַּיְלָה מלה:

*Egypt's firstborn You crushed at midnight. Their host they found not upon arising at night. The army of the prince of Charosheth (Sisra) You swept away with stars of the night. It came to pass at midnight.*

יָעַץ מְחָרֵף לְנוֹפֵף אִוּוּי הוֹבַשְׁתָּ פְגָרָיו בַּלַּיְלָה מלה. כָּרַע
בֵּל וּמַצָּבוֹ בְּאִישׁוֹן לַיְלָה מלה. לְאִישׁ חֲמוּדוֹת נִגְלָה רָז
חֲזוֹת לַיְלָה מלה. וַיְהִי בַּחֲצִי הַלַּיְלָה מלה:

*The blasphemer (Sancheriv) planned to raise his hand against Jerusalem, but You withered his orpses by night. Bel was overturned with its pedestal, in the darkness of night. To the man of Your delight (Daniel) was revealed the mystery of the visions of night. It came to pass at midnight.*

בְּמִשְׁתַּכֵּר בִּכְלֵי קֹדֶשׁ נֶהֱרַג בּוֹ בַּלַּיְלָה מלה. נוֹשַׁע מִבּוֹר

אֲרָיוֹת פּוֹתֵר בִּעֲתוּתֵי לַיְלָה מלה. שִׂנְאָה נָטַר אֲגָגִי וְכָתַב

סְפָרִים בַּלַּיְלָה מלה. וַיְהִי בַּחֲצִי הַלַּיְלָה מלה:

*He (Belshatzar), who caroused from the holy vessels, was killed that very night. From the lion's den was rescued he (Daniel) who interpreted the "terrors" of the night. The Agagite (Haman) nursed hatred and wrote decrees at night. It came to pass at midnight.*

עוֹרַרְתָּ נִצְחֲךָ עָלָיו בְּנֶדֶד שְׁנַת לַיְלָה מלה. פּוּרָה תִדְרוֹךְ

לְשׁוֹמֵר מַה מ"ה מִלַּיְלָה מלה. צָרַח כַּשּׁוֹמֵר וְשָׂח אָתָא בֹקֶר

וְגַם לַיְלָה מלה. וַיְהִי בַּחֲצִי הַלַּיְלָה מלה:

*You began Your triumph over him, when You disturbed (Ahashverosh's) sleep at night. Trample the wine-press to help those who ask the watchman: "What of the long night?" He will shout like a watchman and say: "Morning shall come after night." It came to pass at midnight.*

קָרֵב יוֹם גנד, ח אֲשֶׁר הוּא לֹא יוֹם גנד, ח וְלֹא לַיְלָה מלה. רָם

הוֹדַע כִּי לְךָ הַיּוֹם גנד, ח אַף לְךָ הַלַּיְלָה מלה. שׁוֹמְרִים

הַפְקֵד לְעִירְךָ כָּל ילי הַיּוֹם גנד, ח וְכָל הַלַּיְלָה מלה. תָּאִיר

כְּאוֹר הנ יוֹם גנד, ח וְשֶׁכַת לַיְלָה מלה. וַיְהִי בַּחֲצִי הַלַּיְלָה מלה:

*Hasten the day (of Mashiach), that is neither day nor night. Most High, make known that Yours are day and night. Most High, make known that Yours are day and night. Brighten like the light of day the darkness of night. It came to pass at midnight.*

## UVCHEN

This song connects us to the sacrifices made in the temple 2,000 years ago. Because there is no time, space, or motion, this song transcends these illusionary limitations and delivers the energy of the temple into our hands right now.

וּבְכֵן ע"ב וַאֲמַרְתֶּם זֶבַח פֶּסַח:

*And you shall say: "This is the feast of Passover."*

אוֹמֶץ גְּבוּרוֹתֶיךָ הִפְלֵאתָ בַּפֶּסַח. בְּרֹאשׁ כָּל יּיֹ מוֹעֲדוֹת

נִשֵּׂאתָ פֶּסַח. גִּלִּיתָ לְאֶזְרָחִי וַחֲצוֹת לֵיל פֶּסַח.

וַאֲמַרְתֶּם זֶבַח פֶּסַח:

*And you shall say: "This is the feast of Passover." Above all festivals You elevated Passover. To the Oriental (Abraham) You revealed the future midnight of Passover. And you shall say: "This is the feast of Passover."*

דְּלָתָיו דָּפַקְתָּ כְּחֹם הַיּוֹם ﬡﬞ﬩, בַּפֶּסַח. הִסְעִיד נוֹצְצִים

עֻגּוֹת מַצּוֹת בַּפֶּסַח. וְאֶל הַבָּקָר רָץ זֵכֶר לְשׁוֹר עֵרֶךְ פֶּסַח.

וַאֲמַרְתֶּם זֶבַח פֶּסַח:

*At his door You knocked in the heat of the day on Passover. He satiated the angels with Matzah-cakes on Passover. And he ran to the herd, symbolic of the sacrificial beast of Passover. And you shall say: "This is the feast of Passover."*

זוֹעֲמוּ סְדוֹמִים וְלֹהֲטוּ בָּאֵשׁ בַּפֶּסַח. וְחֻלַּץ לוֹט מֵהֶם

וּמַצּוֹת אָפָה בְּקֵץ פֶּסַח. טִאטֵאתָ אַדְמַת מוֹף וְנוֹף

בְּעָבְרְךָ בַּפֶּסַח. וַאֲמַרְתֶּם זֶבַח פֶּסַח:

*The Sodomites provoked (God) and were devoured by fire on Passover. Lot was withdrawn from them and he baked Matzah at the time of the end of Passover. You swept clean the soil of Moph and Noph (in Egypt) when You passed through on Passover. And you shall say: "This is the feast of Passover."*

יָהּ רֹאשׁ כָּל יּיֹ אוֹן מָחַצְתָּ בְּלֵיל שִׁמּוּר פֶּסַח. כַּבִּיר עַל

בֵּן בְּכוֹר פָּסַחְתָּ בְּדַם פֶּסַח. לְבִלְתִּי תֵּת מַשְׁחִית לָבֹא

בִּפְתָחַי בַּפֶּסַח. וַאֲמַרְתֶּם זֶבַח פֶּסַח:

*O God, You crushed every firstborn of On (in Egypt) on the watchful night of Passover. But Master, Your own firstborn You skipped by merit of the blood of Passover, not to allow the Destroyer to enter my doors on Passover. And you shall say: "This is the feast of Passover."*

מִסְגֶּרֶת סֻגְּרָה בְּעִתּוֹתֵי פֶסַח. נִשְׁמְדָה מִדְיָן בִּצְלִיל

שְׂעוֹרֵי עוֹמֶר פֶסַח. שׂוֹרְפוּ מִשְׁמַנֵּי פוּל וְלוּד בִּיקַד יְקוֹד

פֶסַח. וַאֲמַרְתֶּם זֶבַח פֶּסַח:

*The beleaguered (Jericho) was besieged on Passover. Midian was destroyed at the sound of Omer barley on Passover. The mighty nobles of Pul and Lud (Assyria) Were consumed in a great conflagration on Passover. And you shall say: "This is the feast of Passover."*

עוֹד הַיּוֹם נֹב,יז בְּנֹב לַעֲמוֹד עַד גָּעָה עוֹנַת פֶסַח. פַּס יָד

כָּתְבָה לְקַעֲקֵעַ צוּל בַּפֶּסַח. צָפֹה הַצָּפִית עָרוֹךְ הַשֻּׁלְחָן

בַּפֶּסַח. וַאֲמַרְתֶּם זֶבַח פֶּסַח:

*He (Sancheriv) would have stood that day at Nov, but for the advent of Passover. A hand inscribed the destruction of Zul (Babylon) on Passover. As the watch was set, and the royal table decked on Passover. And you shall say: "This is the feast of Passover."*

קָהָל כִּנְּסָה הֲדַסָּה צוֹם לְשַׁלֵּשׁ בַּפֶּסַח. רֹאשׁ מִבֵּית רָשָׁע

מָחַצְתָּ בְּעֵץ וַחֲמִשִּׁים בַּפֶּסַח. שְׁתֵּי אֵלֶּה רֶגַע תָּבִיא לְעוּצִית

בַּפֶּסַח. תָּעֹז יָדְךָ וְתָרוּם יְמִינֶךָ כְּלֵיל הִתְקַדֵּשׁ חַג פֶּסַח.

וַאֲמַרְתֶּם זֶבַח פֶּסַח:

*Hadassah (Esther) gathered a congregation for a three-day fast on Passover. You caused the head of the evil clan (Haman) to be hanged on a fifty-cubit gallows on Passover. Doubly, will you bring in an instant upon Utzith (Edom) on Passover. Let Your hand be strong, and Your right arm exalted, as on the night when You hallowed the festival of Passover. And you shall say: "This is the feast of Passover."*

### KI LO

This song speaks about God's kingdom, referring to the concept of a king and his subjects. A king cannot be a king without subjects and a kingdom. It is the subjects who help define the king and give him something to rule over. There is a mutual dependency. With God, however, there is no dependency upon anything. Therefore, all God's actions are purely out of love for us. He does not need us. He does not require us to give him reality. No one can dethrone him. We should appreciate this relationship and the infinite love that God has for humanity. To be a subject of the king in this type of situation is a rare privilege, for it is a relationship built upon the greatest of all love – unconditional.

כִּי לוֹ נָאֶה. כִּי לוֹ יָאֶה:

אַדִּיר הוּ בִּמְלוּכָה. בָּחוּר כַּהֲלָכָה. גְּדוּדָיו יֹאמְרוּ לוֹ:

לְךָ וּלְךָ. לְךָ כִּי לְךָ. לְךָ אַף לְךָ. לְךָ יְהֹוָֽאֲדֹנָֽיֵאֲהֹדֹנָהִי

הַמַּמְלָכָה. כִּי לוֹ נָאֶה. כִּי לוֹ יָאֶה:

*To It praise is due! To It praise is fitting! Powerful in majesty, perfectly distinguished, Its regiments of angels say to It: Yours and only Yours; Yours, yet Yours; Yours, surely Yours; Yours Hashem, is the sovereignty. To It praise is due! To It praise is fitting!*

דָּגוּל בִּמְלוּכָה. הָדוּר כַּהֲלָכָה. וָתִיקָיו יֹאמְרוּ לוֹ: לְךָ

וּלְךָ. לְךָ כִּי לְךָ. לְךָ אַף לְךָ. לְךָ יְהֹוָֽאֲדֹנָֽיֵאֲהֹדֹנָהִי הַמַּמְלָכָה.

כִּי לוֹ נָאֶה. כִּי לוֹ יָאֶה:

*Supreme in kingship, perfectly glorious, Its faithful say to It: Yours and only Yours; Yours, yet Yours; Yours, surely Yours; Yours Hashem, is the sovereignty. To It praise is due! To It praise is fitting!*

זַכַּאי בִּמְלוּכָה. וְזִסִין כַּהֲלָכָה. טַפְסְרָיו יֹאמְרוּ לוֹ: לְךָ

וּלְךָ. לְךָ כִּי לְךָ. לְךָ אַף לְךָ. לְךָ יְהֹוָֽאֲדֹנָֽיֵאֲהֹדֹנָהִי הַמַּמְלָכָה.

כִּי לוֹ נָאֶה. כִּי לוֹ יָאֶה:

*Pure in kingship, perfectly immune, Its angels say to It: Yours and only Yours; Yours, yet Yours; Yours, surely Yours; Yours Hashem, is the sovereignty. To It praise is due! To It praise is fitting!*

יָחִיד בִּמְלוּכָה. כַּבִּיר כַּהֲלָכָה. לִמּוּדָיו יֹאמְרוּ לוֹ: לְךָ

וּלְךָ. לְךָ כִּי לְךָ. לְךָ אַף לְךָ. לְךָ יְהֹוָֽאֲדֹנָֽיֵאֲהֹדֹנָהִי הַמַּמְלָכָה.

כִּי לוֹ נָאֶה. כִּי לוֹ יָאֶה:

*Alone in kingship, perfectly omnipotent, Its scholars say to It: Yours and only Yours; Yours, yet Yours; Yours, surely Yours; Yours Hashem, is the sovereignty. To It praise is due! To It praise is fitting!*

מֶלֶךְ בִּמְלוּכָה. נוֹרָא כַּהֲלָכָה. סְבִיבָיו יֹאמְרוּ לוֹ: לְךָ

וּלְךָ. לְךָ כִּי לְךָ. לְךָ אַף לְךָ. לְךָ יְהֹוָהֲאֲדֹנָיאֲדֹנָֽיאַתָּהדֹנֵי הַמַּמְלָכָה.

כִּי לוֹ נָאֶה. כִּי לוֹ יָאֶה:

*Commanding in kingship, perfectly wondrous, Its surroundings say to It: Yours and only Yours; Yours, yet Yours; Yours, surely Yours; Yours Hashem, is the sovereignty. To It praise is due! To It praise is fitting!*

עָנָיו בִּמְלוּכָה. פּוֹדֶה כַּהֲלָכָה. צַדִּיקָיו יֹאמְרוּ לוֹ: לְךָ

וּלְךָ. לְךָ כִּי לְךָ. לְךָ אַף לְךָ. לְךָ יְהֹוָהֲאֲדֹנָיאֲדֹנָֽיאַתָּהדֹנֵי הַמַּמְלָכָה.

כִּי לוֹ נָאֶה. כִּי לוֹ יָאֶה:

*Humble in kingship, perfectly redeeming, Its righteous say to It: Yours and only Yours; Yours, yet Yours; Yours, surely Yours; Yours Hashem, is the sovereignty. To It praise is due! To It praise is fitting!*

קָדוֹשׁ בִּמְלוּכָה. רַחוּם כַּהֲלָכָה. שִׁנְאַנָּיו יֹאמְרוּ לוֹ: לְךָ

וּלְךָ. לְךָ כִּי לְךָ. לְךָ אַף לְךָ. לְךָ יְהֹוָהֲאֲדֹנָיאֲדֹנָֽיאַתָּהדֹנֵי הַמַּמְלָכָה.

כִּי לוֹ נָאֶה. כִּי לוֹ יָאֶה:

*Holy in kingship, perfectly merciful, Its troops of angels say to It: Yours and only Yours; Yours, yet Yours; Yours, surely Yours; Yours Hashem, is the sovereignty. To It praise is due! To It praise is fitting!*

תַּקִּיף בִּמְלוּכָה. תּוֹמֵךְ כַּהֲלָכָה. תְּמִימָיו יֹאמְרוּ לוֹ: לְךָ

וּלְךָ. לְךָ כִּי לְךָ. לְךָ אַף לְךָ. לְךָ יְהֹוָהֲאֲדֹנָיאֲדֹנָֽיאַתָּהדֹנֵי הַמַּמְלָכָה.

כִּי לוֹ נָאֶה. כִּי לוֹ יָאֶה:

*Assertive in kingship, perfectly sustaining, Its perfect ones say to It: Yours and only Yours; Yours, yet Yours; Yours, surely Yours; Yours Hashem, is the sovereignty. To It praise is due! To It praise is fitting!*

## ADIR

This song connects us to the absence of the physical temple. The Creator wants to give us *everything* but cannot because we don't have the vessel of the temple to manifest it.[65] We

---

67. Gazing at a photograph of earth from space reveals a profound Kabbalistic principle concerning the secret to generating spiritual Light. The earth illuminates like a sparkling blue jewel while the space

must feel God's pain and frustration at not being able to impart this fulfillment to us. This will, in turn, motivate us to continually change our nature. Changing our nature is how we build our own internal vessel to receive and thus illuminate God's infinite Light.

אַדִּיר הרי הוּא יִבְנֶה בֵּיתוֹ ב"פ ראה בְּקָרוֹב. בִּמְהֵרָה בִּמְהֵרָה

בְּיָמֵינוּ בְּקָרוֹב. אֵל בְּנֵה. אֵל בְּנֵה. בְּנֵה בֵיתְךָ ב"פ ראה

בְּקָרוֹב:

*It is most mighty. May It soon rebuild Its House, speedily, yes, speedily, in our days, soon. God, rebuild, God, rebuild, rebuild Your House soon.*

בָּחוּר הוּא. גָּדוֹל הוּא. דָּגוּל הוּא. יִבְנֶה בֵיתוֹ ב"פ ראה

בְּקָרוֹב. בִּמְהֵרָה בִּמְהֵרָה בְּיָמֵינוּ בְּקָרוֹב. אֵל בְּנֵה. אֵל

בְּנֵה. בְּנֵה בֵיתְךָ ב"פ ראה בְּקָרוֹב:

*It is distinguished. It is great. It is exalted. May It soon rebuild Its House, speedily, yes, speedily, in our days, soon. God, rebuild, God, rebuild, rebuild Your House soon.*

הָדוּר הוּא. וָתִיק הוּא. זַכַּאי הוּא. וְחָסִיד הוּא. יִבְנֶה בֵיתוֹ

ב"פ ראה בְּקָרוֹב. בִּמְהֵרָה בִּמְהֵרָה בְּיָמֵינוּ בְּקָרוֹב. אֵל בְּנֵה.

אֵל בְּנֵה. בְּנֵה בֵיתְךָ ב"פ ראה בְּקָרוֹב:

*It is all glorious. It is faithful. It is faultless. It is righteous. May It soon rebuild Its House, speedily, yes, speedily, in our days, soon. God, rebuild, God, rebuild, rebuild Your House soon.*

טָהוֹר י"פ אכא הוּא. יָחִיד הוּא. כַּבִּיר הוּא. לִמּוּד הוּא.

מֶלֶךְ הוּא. יִבְנֶה בֵיתוֹ ב"פ ראה בְּקָרוֹב. בִּמְהֵרָה בִּמְהֵרָה

בְּיָמֵינוּ בְּקָרוֹב.

*It is pure. It is unique. It is powerful. It is all-wise. It is King. May It soon rebuild Its House, speedily, yes, speedily, in our days, soon.*

---

around the earth remains black. The reason is, there is no Vessel, no physical object around the earth to reflect the light. Sunlight fills the vacuum of space, but it remains concealed without a Vessel to make it shine. The moment a Vessel reflects the light, an illumination occurs. Likewise, the Creator requires a Vessel to "reflect" His energy in order to generate the Light of fulfillment. The temple was the most powerful Vessel on the planet for generating spiritual Light.

אֵל בְּנֵה. אֵל בְּנֵה. בְּנֵה בֵיתְךָ ב״פ ראה בְּקָרוֹב:

*God, rebuild, God, rebuild, rebuild Your House soon.*

נוֹרָא הוּא. שַׂגִּיב הוּא. עִזּוּז הוּא. פּוֹדֶה הוּא. צַדִּיק הוּא.

יִבְנֵה בֵיתוֹ ב״פ ראה בְּקָרוֹב. בִּמְהֵרָה בִּמְהֵרָה בְּיָמֵינוּ

בְּקָרוֹב. אֵל בְּנֵה. אֵל בְּנֵה. בְּנֵה בֵיתְךָ ב״פ ראה בְּקָרוֹב:

*It is awesome. It is sublime. It is all-powerful. It is the Redeemer. It is righteous. May It soon rebuild Its House, speedily, yes, speedily, in our days, soon. God, rebuild, God, rebuild, rebuild Your House soon.*

קָדוֹשׁ הוּא. רַחוּם הוּא. שַׁדַּי הוּא. תַּקִּיף הוּא. יִבְנֶה

בֵיתוֹ ב״פ ראה בְּקָרוֹב. בִּמְהֵרָה בִּמְהֵרָה בְּיָמֵינוּ בְּקָרוֹב. אֵל

בְּנֵה. אֵל בְּנֵה. בְּנֵה בֵיתְךָ ב״פ ראה בְּקָרוֹב:

*It is holy. It is compassionate. It is Almighty. It is omnipotent. May It soon rebuild Its House, speedily, yes, speedily, in our days, soon. God, rebuild, God, rebuild, rebuild Your House soon.*

### ECHAD MI YODEA

This song takes us on a journey through the numbers one through 13. In the literal song, each number is given its own significance. But there lies a deeper significance to the number 13. Thirteen is a direct reference to the 13 Attributes of God.[66]

אֶחָד אהבה מִי יל׳ יוֹדֵעַ.

*Who knows one?*

אֶחָד אהבה אֲנִי אני יוֹדֵעַ. אֶחָד אהבה אֱלֹהֵינוּ ילה שֶׁבַּשָּׁמַיִם י״פ טל

וּבָאָרֶץ:

*I know one: One is our God, in heaven and on earth.*

---

68. The 13 Attributes are 13 virtues or properties that reflect 13 aspects of our relationship with the Creator. These 13 Attributes are how we interact with God in our daily lives, whether we know it or not. They work like a mirror. When we look into a mirror and smile, the image smiles back. When we look into a mirror and curse, the image curses back. If we perform a negative action in our world, the mirror reflects negative energy at us. There are 13 Attributes that have these reflecting properties within us. As we attempt to transform our reactive nature into proactive, this feedback directs, guides, and corrects us. The number 13 also represents one above the 12 signs of the zodiac. The 12 signs control our instinctive, reactive nature. The number 13 gives us control over the 12 signs, which, in essence, gives us control over our behavior.

שְׁנַיִם מִי יְלֹ יוֹדֵעַ.

*Who knows two?*

שְׁנַיִם אֲנִי אֵי יוֹדֵעַ שְׁנֵי לוּחוֹת הַבְּרִית. אֶחָד אהבה אֱלֹהֵינוּ ילה שֶׁבַּשָּׁמַיִם י"פ טל וּבָאָרֶץ:

*I know two: Two are the Tablets of the Covenant; one is our God, in heaven and on earth.*

שְׁלֹשָׁה מִי יְלֹ יוֹדֵעַ.

*Who knows three?*

שְׁלֹשָׁה אֲנִי אֵי יוֹדֵעַ. שְׁלֹשָׁה אָבוֹת.

*I know three: Three are the Patriarchs;*

שְׁנֵי לוּחוֹת הַבְּרִית. אֶחָד אהבה אֱלֹהֵינוּ ילה שֶׁבַּשָּׁמַיִם י"פ טל וּבָאָרֶץ:

*two are the Tablets of the Covenant; one is our God, in heaven and on earth.*

אַרְבַּע מִי יְלֹ יוֹדֵעַ.

*Who knows four?*

אַרְבַּע אֲנִי אֵי יוֹדֵעַ. אַרְבַּע אִמָּהוֹת. שְׁלֹשָׁה אָבוֹת. שְׁנֵי לוּחוֹת הַבְּרִית. אֶחָד אהבה אֱלֹהֵינוּ ילה שֶׁבַּשָּׁמַיִם י"פ טל וּבָאָרֶץ:

*I know four: Four are the Matriarchs; three are the Patriarchs; two are the Tablets of the Covenant; one is our God, in heaven and on earth.*

וַחֲמִשָּׁה מִי יְלֹ יוֹדֵעַ.

*Who knows five?*

וַחֲמִשָּׁה אֲנִי אֵי יוֹדֵעַ. וַחֲמִשָּׁה וַחֻמְשֵׁי תוֹרָה. אַרְבַּע אִמָּהוֹת. שְׁלֹשָׁה אָבוֹת. שְׁנֵי לוּחוֹת הַבְּרִית. אֶחָד אהבה אֱלֹהֵינוּ ילה שֶׁבַּשָּׁמַיִם י"פ טל וּבָאָרֶץ:

*I know five: Five are the Books of Torah; four are the Matriarchs; three are the Patriarchs; two are the Tablets of the Covenant; one is our God, in heaven and on earth.*

שִׁשָּׁה מִי יכ׳ יוֹדֵעַ.

*Who knows six?*

שִׁשָּׁה אֲנִי אני יוֹדֵעַ. שִׁשָּׁה סִדְרֵי מִשְׁנָה. חֲמִשָּׁה וֹחוּמְשֵׁי תוֹרָה. אַרְבַּע אִמָּהוֹת. שְׁלֹשָׁה אָבוֹת. שְׁנֵי לוּחוֹת הַבְּרִית. אֶחָד אהבה אֱלֹהֵינוּ יכה שֶׁבַּשָּׁמַיִם י"פ טל וּבָאָרֶץ:

*I know six: Six are the Orders of the Mishnah; five are the Books of Torah; four are the Matriarchs; three are the Patriarchs; two are the Tablets of the Covenant; one is our God, in heaven and on earth.*

שִׁבְעָה מִי יכ׳ יוֹדֵעַ.

*Who knows seven?*

שִׁבְעָה אֲנִי אני יוֹדֵעַ. שִׁבְעָה יְמֵי שַׁבַּתָּא. שִׁשָּׁה סִדְרֵי מִשְׁנָה. חֲמִשָּׁה וֹחוּמְשֵׁי תוֹרָה. אַרְבַּע אִמָּהוֹת. שְׁלֹשָׁה אָבוֹת. שְׁנֵי לוּחוֹת הַבְּרִית. אֶחָד אהבה אֱלֹהֵינוּ יכה שֶׁבַּשָּׁמַיִם י"פ טל וּבָאָרֶץ:

*I know seven: Seven are the days of the week; six are the Orders of the Mishnah; five are the Books of Torah; four are the Matriarchs; three are the Patriarchs; two are the Tablets of the Covenant; one is our God, in heaven and on earth.*

שְׁמוֹנָה מִי יכ׳ יוֹדֵעַ.

*Who knows eight?*

שְׁמוֹנָה אֲנִי אני יוֹדֵעַ. שְׁמוֹנָה יְמֵי מִילָה. שִׁבְעָה יְמֵי שַׁבַּתָּא. שִׁשָּׁה סִדְרֵי מִשְׁנָה. חֲמִשָּׁה וֹחוּמְשֵׁי תוֹרָה. אַרְבַּע אִמָּהוֹת. שְׁלֹשָׁה אָבוֹת. שְׁנֵי לוּחוֹת הַבְּרִית. אֶחָד אהבה אֱלֹהֵינוּ יכה שֶׁבַּשָּׁמַיִם י"פ טל וּבָאָרֶץ:

*I know eight: Eight are the days of circumcision; seven are the days of the week; six are the Orders of the Mishnah; five are the Books of Torah; four are the Matriarchs; three are the Patriarchs; two are the Tablets of the Covenant; one is our God, in heaven and on earth.*

תִּשְׁעָה מִי יֹי יוֹדֵעַ.

*Who knows nine?*

תִּשְׁעָה אֲנִי אֲיֹי יוֹדֵעַ. תִּשְׁעָה יַרְחֵי לֵידָה. שְׁמוֹנָה יְמֵי
מִילָה. שִׁבְעָה יְמֵי שַׁבַּתָּא. שִׁשָּׁה סִדְרֵי מִשְׁנָה. וַחֲמִשָּׁה
ווּמְשֵׁי תוֹרָה. אַרְבַּע אִמָּהוֹת. שְׁלֹשָׁה אָבוֹת. שְׁנֵי לֻוחוֹת
הַבְּרִית. אֶחָד אהבה אֱלֹהֵינוּ ילה שֶׁבַּשָּׁמַיִם יֹפ טל וּבָאָרֶץ:

*I know nine: Nine are the months of pregnancy; eight are the days of circumcision; seven are the days of the week; six are the Orders of the Mishnah; five are the Books of Torah; four are the Matriarchs; three are the Patriarchs; two are the Tablets of the Covenant; one is our God, in heaven and on earth.*

עֲשָׂרָה מִי יֹי יוֹדֵעַ.

*Who knows ten?*

עֲשָׂרָה אֲנִי אֲיֹי יוֹדֵעַ. עֲשָׂרָה דִבְּרַיָא. תִּשְׁעָה יַרְחֵי לֵידָה.
שְׁמוֹנָה יְמֵי מִילָה. שִׁבְעָה יְמֵי שַׁבַּתָּא. שִׁשָּׁה סִדְרֵי
מִשְׁנָה. וַחֲמִשָּׁה ווּמְשֵׁי תוֹרָה. אַרְבַּע אִמָּהוֹת. שְׁלֹשָׁה
אָבוֹת. שְׁנֵי לֻוחוֹת הַבְּרִית. אֶחָד אהבה אֱלֹהֵינוּ ילה
שֶׁבַּשָּׁמַיִם יֹפ טל וּבָאָרֶץ:

*I know ten: ten are the ten Commandments; nine are the months of pregnancy; eight are the days of circumcision; seven are the days of the week; six are the Orders of the Mishnah; five are the Books of Torah; four are the Matriarchs; three are the Patriarchs; two are the Tablets of the Covenant; one is our God, in heaven and on earth.*

אַחַד אהבה עָשָׂר מִי יֹי יוֹדֵעַ.

*Who knows eleven?*

אַחַד אהבה עָשָׂר אֲנִי אֲיֹי יוֹדֵעַ. אַחַד אהבה עָשָׂר כּוֹכְבַיָּא.
עֲשָׂרָה דִבְּרַיָא. תִּשְׁעָה יַרְחֵי לֵידָה. שְׁמוֹנָה יְמֵי מִילָה.

*I know eleven: eleven are the stars; ten are the ten Commandments; nine are the months of pregnancy; eight are the days of circumcision;*

שִׁבְעָה יְמֵי שַׁבַּתָּא. שִׁשָּׁה סִדְרֵי מִשְׁנָה. וַחֲמִשָּׁה וֹוּמִשֵׁי
תּוֹרָה. אַרְבַּע אִמָּהוֹת. שְׁלֹשָׁה אָבוֹת. שְׁנֵי לוּחוֹת הַבְּרִית.
אֶוָֹד אהבה אֱלֹהֵינוּ ילה שֶׁבַּשָּׁמַיִם י־פ טל וּבָאָרֶץ:

*four are the Matriarchs; three are the Patriarchs; two are the Tablets of the Covenant; one is our God, in seven days of the week, are the five are the Books of Torah; days of the week; six are the Orders of the Mishnah; heaven and on earth.*

שְׁנֵים עָשָׂר מִי ילי יוֹדֵעַ.

*Who knows twelve?*

שְׁנֵים עָשָׂר אֲנִי אני יוֹדֵעַ. שְׁנֵים עָשָׂר שִׁבְטַיָּא. אַוָֹד עָשָׂר
כּוֹכְבַיָּא. עֲשָׂרָה דִבְּרַיָּא. תִּשְׁעָה יַרְחֵי לֵידָה. שְׁמוֹנָה יְמֵי
מִילָה. שִׁבְעָה יְמֵי שַׁבַּתָּא. שִׁשָּׁה סִדְרֵי מִשְׁנָה. וַחֲמִשָּׁה
וֹוּמִשֵׁי תּוֹרָה. אַרְבַּע אִמָּהוֹת. שְׁלֹשָׁה אָבוֹת. שְׁנֵי לוּחוֹת
הַבְּרִית. אֶוָֹד אהבה אֱלֹהֵינוּ ילה שֶׁבַּשָּׁמַיִם י־פ טל וּבָאָרֶץ:

*I know twelve: twelve are the tribes; eleven are the stars; ten are the ten Commandments; nine are the months of pregnancy; eight are the days of circumcision; seven are the days of the week; six are the Orders of the Mishnah; five are the Books of Torah; four are the Matriarchs; three are the Patriarchs; two are the Tablets of the Covenant; one is our God, in heaven and on earth.*

שְׁלֹשָׁה עָשָׂר מִי ילי יוֹדֵעַ.

*Who knows thirteen?*

שְׁלֹשָׁה עָשָׂר אֲנִי אני יוֹדֵעַ. שְׁלֹשָׁה עָשָׂר מִדַּיָּא. שְׁנֵים
עָשָׂר שִׁבְטַיָּא. אַוָֹד עָשָׂר כּוֹכְבַיָּא. עֲשָׂרָה דִבְּרַיָּא.
תִּשְׁעָה יַרְחֵי לֵידָה. שְׁמוֹנָה יְמֵי מִילָה. שִׁבְעָה יְמֵי
שַׁבַּתָּא. שִׁשָּׁה סִדְרֵי מִשְׁנָה.

*I know thirteen: thirteen are the attributes of God; twelve are the tribes; eleven are the stars; ten are the ten Commandments; nine are the months of pregnancy; eight are the days of circumcision; seven are the days of the week; six are the Orders of the Mishnah;*

וַחֲמִשָּׁה וְחוּמְשֵׁי תוֹרָה. אַרְבַּע אִמָּהוֹת. שְׁלֹשָׁה אָבוֹת. שְׁנֵי

לוּחוֹת הַבְּרִית. אֶחָד אהבה אֱלֹהֵינוּ יה שֶׁבַּשָּׁמַיִם יפ טל וּבָאָרֶץ:

*five are the Books of Torah; four are the Matriarchs; three are the Patriarchs; two are the Tablets of the Covenant; one is our God, in heaven and on earth.*

### CHAD GADIA

This song is about a man who buys a goat for a small amount of money. Interestingly, this song is not in Hebrew but Aramaic. The Aramaic language is a code that the angels cannot understand.[67] It is a language that is beyond their comprehension. Because the negative side of Satan also has angels that can influence and sabotage our connections, we employ Aramaic when we want to bypass all angels. In this song, God slaughters the Angel of Death, giving birth to immortality. The power of this song actually connects us, God, and the force of immortality. Therefore, we do not want any negative angels interfering with it. This song also helps release the energy of immortality into our physical world, where it can then manifest through the work of scientists, doctors, and medical researchers.[68]

We must teach our children spiritual values through living examples, for our children always grow up and emulate our true spiritual nature. Words alone will never build character and spiritual values in our loved ones. Their spiritual development is directly influenced by our actions.

חַד גַּדְיָא, חַד גַּדְיָא. דְּזַבִּין אַבָּא בִּתְרֵי זוּזֵי. חַד גַּדְיָא, חַד

גַּדְיָא. וְאָתָא שׁוּנְרָא, וְאָכְלָה לְגַדְיָא, דְּזַבִּין אַבָּא בִּתְרֵי

זוּזֵי. חַד גַּדְיָא, חַד גַּדְיָא.

*A kid, a kid that father bought for two zuzim, a kid, a kid. A cat then came and devoured the kid that father bought for two zuzim, a kid, a kid.*

וְאָתָא כַלְבָּא, וְנָשַׁךְ לְשׁוּנְרָא, דְּאָכְלָה לְגַדְיָא,

דְּזַבִּין אַבָּא בִּתְרֵי זוּזֵי.

חַד גַּדְיָא, חַד גַּדְיָא.

*A dog then came and bit the cat that devoured the kid that father bought for two zuzim, a kid, a kid.*

---

69. Kol Nidre, which is recited on Yom Kippur, the Zohar, the Kaddish, and the Talmud are all written in Aramaic. Marriage certificates are also composed in Aramaic. This protects these holy connections and documents from any negative influences.

70. In 1998, the biotechnology firm Geron announced that it was able to produce immortal human stem cells in the laboratory. Remarkably, these stem cells were found to be immortal.
Tom Okarma, Geron's VP of research and development, said, "The discovery that we are talking about is the derivation of human embryonic stem cells that are capable of developing into all cells and tissues of the body and are immortal. The cells are immortal. They will live forever."

וְאָתָא חוּטְרָא, וְהִכָּה לְכַלְבָּא, דְּנָשַׁךְ לְשׁוּנְרָא,
דְּאָכְלָה לְגַדְיָא, דְּזַבִּין אַבָּא בִּתְרֵי זוּזֵי.
וַד גַּדְיָא, וַד גַּדְיָא.

*A stick then came and beat the dog that bit the cat that devoured the kid that father bought for two zuzim, a kid, a kid.*

וְאָתָא נוּרָא, וְשָׂרַף לְחוּטְרָא, דְּהִכָּה לְכַלְבָּא,
דְּנָשַׁךְ לְשׁוּנְרָא, דְּאָכְלָה לְגַדְיָא,
דְּזַבִּין אַבָּא בִּתְרֵי זוּזֵי.
וַד גַּדְיָא, וַד גַּדְיָא.

*A fire then came and burnt the stick that beat the dog that bit the cat that devoured the kid that father bought for two zuzim, a kid, a kid.*

וְאָתָא מַיָּא, וְכָבָה לְנוּרָא, דְּשָׂרַף לְחוּטְרָא, דְּהִכָּה
לְכַלְבָּא, דְּנָשַׁךְ לְשׁוּנְרָא, דְּאָכְלָה לְגַדְיָא,
דְּזַבִּין אַבָּא בִּתְרֵי זוּזֵי.
וַד גַּדְיָא, וַד גַּדְיָא.

*Water then came and quenched the fire that burnt the stick that beat the dog that bit the cat that devoured the kid that father bought for two zuzim, a kid, a kid.*

וְאָתָא תּוֹרָא, וְשָׁתָה לְמַיָּא, דְּכָבָה לְנוּרָא, דְּשָׂרַף
לְחוּטְרָא, דְּהִכָּה לְכַלְבָּא, דְּנָשַׁךְ לְשׁוּנְרָא, דְּאָכְלָה
לְגַדְיָא, דְּזַבִּין אַבָּא בִּתְרֵי זוּזֵי.
וַד גַּדְיָא, וַד גַּדְיָא.

*An ox then came and drank the water that quenched the fire that burnt the stick that beat the dog that bit the cat that devoured the kid that father bought for two zuzim, a kid, a kid.*

וְאָתָא הַשּׁוֹחֵט, וְשָׁחַט לְתוֹרָא, דְּשָׁתָה לְמַיָּא, דְּכָבָה
לְנוּרָא, דְּשָׂרַף לְחוּטְרָא, דְּהִכָּה לְכַלְבָּא, דְּנָשַׁךְ
לְשׁוּנְרָא, דְּאָכְלָה לְגַּדְיָא, דְּזַבִּין אַבָּא בִּתְרֵי זוּזֵי.
חַד גַּדְיָא, חַד גַּדְיָא.

*A slaughterer then came and slaughtered the ox that drank the water that quenched the fire that burnt the stick that beat the dog that bit the cat that devoured the kid that father bought for two zuzim, a kid, a kid.*

וְאָתָא מַלְאַךְ הַמָּוֶת, וְשָׁחַט לְשׁוֹחֵט, דְּשָׁחַט לְתוֹרָא,
דְּשָׁתָה לְמַיָּא, דְּכָבָה לְנוּרָא, דְּשָׂרַף לְחוּטְרָא, דְּהִכָּה
לְכַלְבָּא, דְּנָשַׁךְ לְשׁוּנְרָא, דְּאָכְלָה לְגַּדְיָא,
דְּזַבִּין אַבָּא בִּתְרֵי זוּזֵי. חַד גַּדְיָא, חַד גַּדְיָא.

*The angel of death then came and killed the slaughterer that slaughtered the ox that drank the water that quenched the fire that burnt the stick that beat the dog that bit the cat that devoured the kid that father bought for two zuzim, a kid, a kid.*

וְאָתָא הַקָּדוֹשׁ בָּרוּךְ הוּא, וְשָׁחַט לְמַלְאַךְ הַמָּוֶת דְּשָׁחַט
לְשׁוֹחֵט, דְּשָׁחַט לְתוֹרָא, דְּשָׁתָה לְמַיָּא, דְּכָבָה לְנוּרָא,
דְּשָׂרַף לְחוּטְרָא, דְּהִכָּה לְכַלְבָּא, דְּנָשַׁךְ לְשׁוּנְרָא,
דְּאָכְלָה לְגַּדְיָא, דְּזַבִּין אַבָּא בִּתְרֵי זוּזֵי.
חַד גַּדְיָא, חַד גַּדְיָא.

*The Holy One, Blessed be He, then came and slew the angel of death that killed the slaughterer that slaughtered the ox that drank the water that quenched the fire that burnt the stick that beat the dog that bit the cat that devoured the kid that father bought for two zuzim, a kid, a kid.*

# THE UPPER TRIANGLE

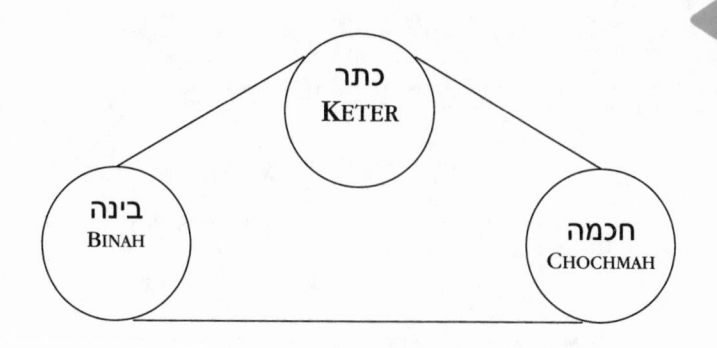

# THE SEVEN SFIROT
### ZEIR ANPIN (6) + MALCHUT(1)

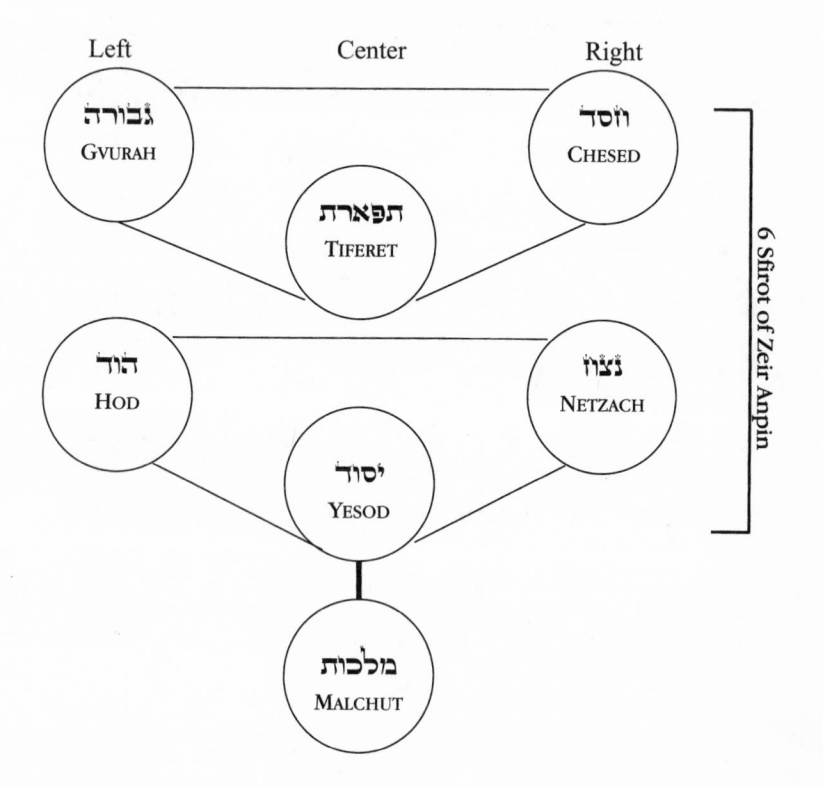

## THE TEN SFIROT

In order to conceal the blazing Light of the Endless from us, a series of curtains were put up. Ten "curtains" were used to conceal the Light.

Each successive curtain further reduces the emanation of Light, gradually dimming its brilliance to a level that is almost imperceivable to our five senses. The result is our darkened universe of chaos. We now have an arena suitable to play the game of life.

These ten curtains are known as the **ten Sfirot**

The ten Sfirot embody many more elements than will be discussed here. Because this subject could fill a 24 volume encyclopedia, all the elements cannot be explained here in detail. Rather, here are the essential characteristics and attributes of the Ten as they apply in the world in which we dwell:

### KETER

Keter, which sits like a Crown at the top, above the central column, contains all the incarnations of all the souls in existence. It embodies God as unknown and unknowable and is located just below the Endless World of limitless Light, so far removed from mortal comprehension that its direct effect upon our lives is negligible.

Still, Keter is the blazing intelligence that channels the Lightforce of Creation to the rest of the Sfirot. It functions as a super-computer, containing the total inventory of what each of us is, ever has been or ever will be. As such, it is the genesis not only of our lives in this earth realm, but of every thought, idea or inspiration we ever will have while we sojourn here -- all of which brings us to a necessary aside on the subject of multiple lifetimes, past, present and future.

Reincarnation, in which the human soul returns to this realm again and again until its imperfections are corrected, is a central tenet of Kabbalah.

This correction process is called Tikkun. Other spiritual teachings refer to the Tikkun process as Karma.

The process, in which a soul is channeled down through the Ten Sfirot to be born in the physical portion of Malchut, begins in Keter, and no soul leaves there without the baggage it has accrued in previous lifetimes.

Unlike the occasional flight aboard a major airline in which you wind up in New York while your baggage goes to Bangkok, Tikkun baggage always arrives at its proper destination. You couldn't lose it in transit even if you wanted to because the sole purpose of your journey here is to leave it right here when once again it is time to pass through the illusory door called death. Most souls can lose their self-imposed burdens of Tikkun debt only through repeated trips to this plane of existence.

The light of Keter has a long way to go before it reaches us. It is as far removed from the physical realm in which we live as an architect's first thought is removed from the building that that thought will ultimately become.

Keter is the source of everything, but only in undifferentiated potential. The rest of the Sfirot are needed to turn that potential into something we can perceive as reality, and the first to receive the power flowing out of Keter is...

### CHOCHMAH

Chochmah, at the top of the right-hand column, is the first depot containing all the Wisdom in the universe. Chochmah represents the beginning of the Zodiac. It contains the totality of the Light, and stands as the universal father-figure. But Wisdom, passively contemplating itself alone in a warehouse, is of no value on any plane of existence. To be of use, it must be inventoried, shipped out and supplied to those in need of it. To accomplish that, Chochmah requires connection with its corresponding mother-figure, which is...

## BINAH

Binah, at the top of the left-hand column, represents Understanding.

Binah is a powerhouse of cosmic energy. In fact, even as Chochmah encapsulates all wisdom, Binah contains all energy, from that which motivates human endeavor and tugs at Earthly tides to that which keeps galaxies spinning and stars burning. When thought must be made manifest in action, Chochmah and Binah meet, combine their energies, and transform raw information into knowledge.

In other words, Chochmah can be likened to a simpleton who carries an encyclopedia on his back. Possession of the encyclopedia does not make the man smarter. Binah internalizes the content so that information actually becomes knowledge and part of the person.

## CHESED

Chesed, the most expansive of the Sfirot, representing Mercy, sits below Chochmah on the right-hand column. Chesed, representing pure positive energy, holds the still undifferentiated seed of all that has taken place between Chochmah and Binah, and since it represents the total Desire to Share, it can be generous to a fault.

We all have seen Chesed run amok. It is the ultra-liberal who weeps more for the criminal than for his victim; it is the poor man who wins the lottery and gives every penny of his new fortune to charity, leaving his own family destitute. Unrestrained, Chesed gives until it hurts -- *almost everybody*. Fortunately, Chesed does have a balancing counterpart, just across the way, on the left-hand column, right under Binah. It is called...

## Gvurah

Gvurah is known as Judgment. Whereas Chesed gives almost to a fault, Gvurah is miserly. Where Chesed expands, Gvurah contracts.

Where Chesed says, "Share," Gvurah says "What's in it for me?"

Where Chesed celebrates heroism, Gvurah is a disciplinarian with fear looking over its shoulder.

Gvurah, run amok, without Chesed 's balance, becomes the tyranny of a police state. But even as Chochmah's Wisdom cannot become manifest without Binah's energy and understanding, neither can the undifferentiated seed that lies in Chesed ever become the differentiated tree without Gvurah's strong hand.

That which Chochmah and Binah have put together and passed down to Chesed, Gvurah brings into differentiation, which is the beginning of physicality. This process is not as complicated as it might seem at first glance.

## TIFERET

Tiferet, representing Beauty, rests below Keter on the central column, and beneath Chesed and Gvurah to the right and left. Tiferet is Beauty because a thing of beauty, whether a sunset, a flower, a poem or a human mind, must combine wisdom [Chochmah], understanding [Binah] and the luminosity of the Light to exist as such.

Tiferet also is a thing of beauty because it is the balancing point between right and left columns, and without the symmetry of balance, there can be no beauty. Tiferet, thus contains all aspects of the world in which we live. Tiferet teaches us when to share and when to receive. Tiferet represents that elusive balance between judgment and mercy that allows a parent to discipline their child out of love instead of out of reactive anger.

### NETZACH

Netzach, or Victory, resides on the right-hand column, just below Chesed. A repository and storehouse of positive energy from Chesed, Netzach radiates the *Desire to Share* and becomes the channel of that energy as it begins to approach the physical world in which we live.

It is, in short, analogous to the sperm that, in union with the egg, ultimately creates the individual human being. Netzach also represents eternity and involuntary processes and is representative of the right brain where the creative process takes place. Netzach, in short, is the artist, the poet, the musician, the dreamer and the masculine fertilizing principle.

Its feminine counterpart, directly across the way on the left-hand column is...

### HOD

Hod stands for Glory. Hod, analogous to the egg in human conception, begins the materialization of that which was held solely in potential in Chesed /Netzach, much as a woman gives actual birth to that which has been conceived in conjunction with the male fertilizing principle. Hod also controls voluntary processes and left-brain activities, channeling the practicality of Gvurah into the human psyche. As Netzach is the artist, Hod is the scientist, the logician, the math whiz and the Certified Public Accountant in the brown tweed suit.

### YESOD

Yesod, or Foundation, sits like a great reservoir at the bottom of the Ten. All the Sfirot above pour their intellect and their attributes into its vast basin where they are mixed, balanced and made ready for transfer in a radiance so brilliant no mortal could survive in its presence. Metaphorically speaking, Yesod is a cement truck that gathers all the raw compounds including water and sand, blends them together and pours out a wet mixture that will eventually solidify and harden into the cement that is our physical universe, otherwise known as...

### MALCHUT

Malchut, the Kingdom, contains the world of physicality.

It is here where the unconcealed cement mixture hardens like rock and takes on physical form and structure. It is the only one of the Sfirot where physical material seems to exist -- in a minuscule percentage of the whole. And it is here that a divergence in human attitude spells the difference between individual lives lived in the Light, and those lived in darkness.

### THE SIX

The ancient Kabbalists explain that of the above 10 dimensions, 6 in particular [Chesed, Gvurah, Tiferet, Netzach, Hod, and Yesod] are tightly enfolded within each other, compactified in a dimension known cumulatively as Zeir Anpin. [See chart on page 143.]

## SCIENCE, KABBALAH, & SUPERSTRINGS

Interestingly, 20th century physicists revealed an uncanny similar view of our universe with the advent of Superstring Theory. SuperString Theory is an attempt to unify Einstein's theory of relativity with quantum mechanics. According to the theory, all subatomic particles are actually different resonance of tiny vibrating superstrings, much the same way that different musical notes can emanate from a single guitar string.

Superstring theory further contends that our universe must contain ten dimensions in order for it to reconcile with Einstein's theory of relativity and therefore, account for the force of gravity. The ancient Kabbalists unveiled a similar ten dimensional view of the universe some 4000 years ago.

The similarity is intensified in regards to the six Sfirot that are enfolded in the one domain called, Zeir Anpin. Superstring theorist Michio Kaku writing in the journal New Scientist states:

*"The Universe is a symphony of vibrating strings. And when strings move in ten-dimensional space-time, they warp the space-time surrounding them in precisely the way predicted by general relativity.*

Physicists retrieve our more familiar 4-dimensional Universe by assuming that, during the big bang, 6 of the ten dimensions curled up (or "compactified") into a tiny ball, while the remaining four expanded explosively, giving us the Universe we see.

The modern-day scientist and the ancient Kabbalist concur that reality exists in ten dimensions and that 6 dimensions are tightly compacted.